Contents

BY THE WAY

It is a very serious criminal offence for a
publisher to market a book knowing that it
contains less pages than he claims it does.
This copy of Not The General Election
should contain

ΛT LEΛST 120 pages, 68 of them in full
colour and smelling nicely. If your copy is
for any reason a brick short of a load, the
man to sue is Colin Webb at Pavilion
Books.

This book was revealed as a vision to two
Portuguese shepherds in the autumn of
1927, and was previously published in
Madrid, Rome and Manila as Y Septima
Secreti Di Thatima. This edition was
translated from the Portuguese by John
Lloyd and Sean Hardie, with the help of
Laurie Rowley and Colin Gilbert and a
couple of prayers from Phil Differ. The
task of restoring and illustrating the
manuscript was entrusted to the Brothers
of Dewynters the Blessed in Dover Street,
under the devout eye of Monsignor
Anthony Pye Jeary. The
illuminations were lovingly unearthed
by Sister Mary Williams, and are owned
by Camera Press, Syndication
International, Popperfoto, Keystone Press
Agency, Express Newspapers.
and the whole lot copyrighted by those
awfully unpleasant people at Not The
Nine O'Clock News Ltd.

First published in Great Britain
by Sphere Books Ltd 1983

© Not the Nine O'Clock News 1983
Not the Nine O'Clock News is a BBC
Television Production
Published in association with
Pavilion Books

SPHERE

DID

◀ ### Did you know?
National Front leader Martin Webster once attempted to bribe the police with a pound of sausages?

Did you know? ▶
Voting in the Democratic State of Liberia is so secret that the electorate are not even allowed to see where they put their cross.

Did you know?
Sir Geoffrey Howe and his wife Lady Jock pause for pictures after successfully securing the release of Rudolf Hess from Spandau Gaol. ◀

SCOOP. ▶
This is the first picture of Mrs Thatcher together with the secret baby she had on her so called 'tour' of the Falkland Islands. The baby, Mark II, already has his name down for unemployment benefit.

TAKING THE HIS OUT OF HISTORY
Although there are many rival claimants to the title of Founder of Modern Conservatism—Disraeli, Churchill, Macmillan, Princess Anne—it's typical of Mrs Thatcher to have chosen as election day the 400th anniversary of the birth of her great hero Oliver Cromwell. Both were the off-spring of Lincolnshire butchers, both suffered crises of sexual identity in childhood, both share adult obsessions about the size and shape of their ear lobes. Interestingly at her age he had been dead for eighteen months.

Did you know?
That Norman St John Stevas was removed to the obscurity of the back benches because he was always breaking wind on the front ones. ▶

Did you know?
Arthur Scargill, in his capacity as leader of the NUM, is provided with a free PIFCO "Travel Toupee- Corrector" (£9.95 from all good stores).

YOU KNOW?

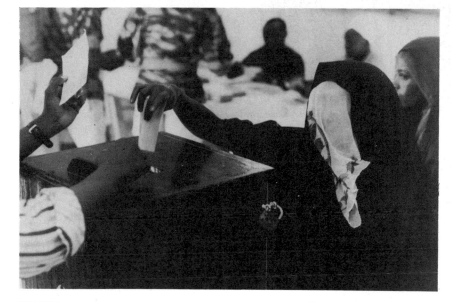

Did you know?
Tony Benn always carries a baby on election campaigns to shield himself from assassin's bullets.

Did you know?
Mrs Thatcher personally signs all deportation orders.

NOT

**A HOPE IN HELL
A CHANCE
A MOMENT TOO SOON
YOU AGAIN
TONIGHT JOSEPHINE
MY CUP OF TEA
NOT WHO'S THERE**

More than 23 million British citizens are unrepresented

So. As you can see. Although, at the last General Election, more than 23,000,000 were NOT voters, they do not possess ONE SINGLE SEAT IN PARLIAMENT—thanks to the outdated and unfair electoral system in this country which favours the small minority and "lunatic" parties.

It makes you wonder what the SDP are whining about, doesn't it?

But at last, all that is changing. Because now *The Not Party* is here to represent *your* interests. As against the interests of the 30,000,000 or so other slimy bastards who got us into this mess by voting for Thatcher, Foot, Martin Webster etc.

The figures above, if translated into this forthcoming election, represent a 173% swing to the Not Party: giving us a 622 seat majority in Parliament *at least*. The Not Party would own over 94% of MPs (entitling us to a fabulous *twelve and a half* Prime Ministers). The Tories, on the other hand, would be wiped off the map: holding only Balmoral (Central) with an estimated majority of 6 votes, and the parts of Aldershot which have barbed wire round them. The Labour Party would retain only Salford (Dosshouse) and Hampstead (Pizza Hut). That and five United Ulster Maniacs would make up the whole House of Commons! WHAT DO I HAVE TO DO TO GET A SLICE OF THIS IMMENSE AMOUNT OF POWER SO THAT I CAN BORE EVERYONE TO DEATH ON TELEVISION, GO TO THE SAME CINEMA THE QUEEN DOES, MAKE "WOOAHH, WAAOOH" NOISES ON 'TODAY IN PARLIAMENT', HELP THE OLD FOLK ETC? The answer is nothing. Sod all. Just fill in the application form

below and wait. Because now THE NOT PARTY, thanks to Channel Four, new legislation, boundary changes etc is entitled to as many seats in Parliament as it wants providing it can prove that it is disabled, lesbian, boring, can't pronounce names properly during continuity announcements etc. And we can. And we will.

As a NOT VOTER you don't even have to *STAND UP AND BE COUNTED*—we've already counted you sitting down and you come to 23,659,610.*

HM Elizabeth Her Majesty The Queen Mother, our beloved honorary patron has NOT voted for 411 years. She will be NOT voting in the next election. We say "cheers" your Majesty Queen Mum and Drive Carefully.

THE COMPANY YOU KEEP
Famous people who were **NOT** voters include:

Jesus	Anne of Cleeves
Buddha	Garner Ted Armstrong
Alexander the Great	William Tell
Charlemagne	Lassie
Robin Hood	Phil the Fluter
Leonardo da Vinci	Princess Michael of Kent
Michaelangelo	James Bond 007
Richard the Lionheart	Simon Templar
Wat Tyler	Mr. Kipling
Princess Diana	Matthew & Son
Vasco da Gama	El Cid
Andrew Lloyd Webber	Bulldog Drummond
Asterix	The Man Who Broke The
Moby Dick	Bank At Monte Carlo
Joan of Arc	Gandhi
Prince William	John Alderton
Dr Snuggles	Dennis Thatcher
The Ran of Kutch	Generl Galtieri
Turnbull & Asser	David Attenborough
Leo the XXIX	Dickie Attenborough
Mott the Hoople	Johnny Mills
Pele	Seany Connery
ET	Frankie Mitterand
Rudolph the Red Nose Reindeer	Andy Andropov
Scott of the Arctic	Mrs Edward Heath
Shergar	The Nigger In The
William Shakespeare	Woodpile

**No. of Voters 1979 General Election
(Source: Whitakers Almanac 1983 Edition)**

Not	23,659,610
Con	13,697,753
Lab	11,506,741
Lib	4,305,324
SNP	504,259
NF	191,706
PC	132,554
Loonies	188,063

Lab. Con. Lib. Not. Oth.

THE VERY TENTATIVE POLICIES OF THE NOT PARTY (*DO* TELL US IF YOU HATE THEM!)

* **End of term exams for teachers**
* **Income tax relief for people who are never ill**
* **Introduction of minimum height requirement of 5'9" for television personalities**
* **No tax on overtime**
* **Abolition of slavery**
* **Real food to be served in hospitals**
* **Normal people to be allowed to stand for Parliament**
* **Porsche drivers to explain to the rest of us how they manage it**
* **Judges to retire at 95**
* **No-one to own a dog unless they own a piece of shitting land more than fourteen times the size of the animal**
* **The words "there's no demand for it" to be made illegal in shops**
* **Proper music to be played in lifts**

*Note: figures exclude Northern Ireland.

23,659,610 CAN NOT BE WRONG?

now in this 'so-called' democracy. Just look at the facts.

THE NOT PARTY MANIFESTO

The Not Party believes that *You* know what *We* think, and not vice versa. That's why what our policies are is very much in *your* hands. Why not write to us telling us how much *you* care about things. The old folk. And so on. We don't pretend to know how many beans make five. But we know about *people*. That's why we've commissioned a special set of N.O.T. sample surveys to let YOU know what the *people* think. Have a look. Mull it over. Let us know.

WHAT THE POLITICIANS THINK THE ISSUES ARE

TOP 10

1 Whether or not the Honourable Member opposite is a liar, fascist, communist, traitor, incontinent, ill-hung, big-eared, drunk, spastic, fatherless, unbuttoned, a dung-eater, impotent, opportunist, a cuckold, wet around the fetlocks, three-nippled, Welsh etc.
2 The Money Supply
3 The Unions/Lack of choice in shoe shops
4 Car parking/The weather
5 The Russians
6 Arthur Scargill's private life
7 The New-Look ''Punch''
8 How impossible it is not to sympathise with the unemployed
9 The Moral Decline of the Young
10 The outcome of the Guatemalan elections/Simon Hoggart

BOTTOM 10

1 Poverty
2 The fact that most of the world is starving
3 Smoking/Alcoholism
4 Britain's role in the international arms trade
5 Angela Rippon's Favourite Garden Furniture
6 A date for withdrawal from Ulster

7 Nick Heywood's prospects as a solo performer
8 Modern architecture/Long term unemployment
9 What happens to TVam
10 The possibility that we've made some mistakes

Survey based on a random sample of back numbers of Hansard over the past 5 years, adjusted to take account of the massive laundering operation which goes on before speeches and interruptions get into print.

THE *ACTUAL* ISSUES

Digest of the ten most important facts in the galaxy compiled from the reports of The Houston Institute Of The Extremely Intelligent, The Intergalactic Council of Sirius-B and His Supreme Holiness God Almighty O.B.E.

1 The Danger To Galactic Safety Represented By The Zillons from Tharg-9
2 The Second Coming Of Christ Will Occur on ''The Paul Squire Show'' at 8.42pm on the 15th November 1984 just behind the potted plant
3 The Major Undiagnosed Symptom of Cancer is Wanting To Pee When The Light Goes Out (Squeens Syndrome)
4 A New Kind of V.D. caused by U.H.T. milk is Spreading Down From Norway
5 The Major Threat to World Peace Is Belgium

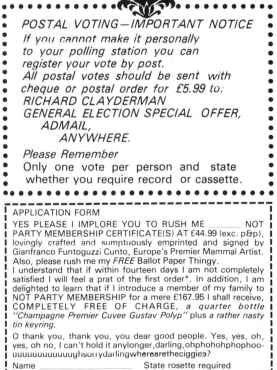

As a special request we print this picture for the 49,000,000 people who want to see the back of Mrs Thatcher.

Saaaaaaaaaatchi & Saaaaaaaaaatchi inc.

June 4th

The Rt Hon Cecil Parkinson
Chairman, Conservative & Unionist Pty
Smith Square
London, W1A 2QT

PRIVATE AND CONFIDENTIAL

Dear Cecil,

Thanks for a most enjoyable and entertaining lunch. Herewith as promised a few preliminary thoughts: perhaps you could pass on where appropriate, and let me have any comments of your own.

1) THE P.M.'S SHOES

Is there a way of broaching this one tactfully? And do they really have to be British? (Last time round we simply did a label-switch on most of the clothing, with no-one any the wiser).

2) WILLIE

Once again imperative that he stears clear of the Press after lunchtime - they like him, but we've had some perilously close misses of late. Also needs to cut back on the "jolly good, splendid, carry on" routine a bit - we're giving alternatives some thought, but it needs to be something he can learn without too much difficulty.

3) PYM

Either a Peerage Or new teeth, don't mind which but soon, please. Injection of dignity a matter of some urgency.

4) PRIOR

Is it feasible to leave him in Ulster throughout?

5) TEBBIT

God knows, Cecil, God knows. I suppose it would help if we could at least get our hands on one photo of him smiling, ideally within a mile or two of a Worker; and get him to stop spitting at people when there are cameramen around. Does he have hobbies? A nice friendly room they could do for the Colour Supps?

6) HOWE

Can we find a less Home Counties pub for him to drink in? Right idea, wrong location. Help too if he could manage a whole pint - the halves can give the wrong impression.

7) HESELTINE

Michael's only problem as MOD is that he doesn't look remotely like a soldier (Peter Walker has the same problem with the farmers). Consequence is that people are apt to get the impression Mike likes the bomb because he's idle, frightened of getting mud on his brogues in a real war. Could you talk to him about it, tactfully?

Continued.....

The Prime Minister demonstrates her famous "you lend me a fiver, I give you back a quid, now you only owe me four" technique to trainee supermar[ket] cashiers.

Mrs T's holiday villa in the Falklands.

.....2.....

8) SIR KEITH

If there's really no possibility of an Early Bath, all I can suggest is that he spends as much time as possible socialising with palpably sane, normal citizens in public places, sharing jokes with footballers etc: and stays clear of speaking engagements at all costs.

9) LEON BRITTAN

Without putting too fine a point on it, he's a bit more gentile if you avoid the profile. Sorry.

10) JOHN BIFFEN

To be quite honest if he was anything other than a politician we'd re-launch him under another brand name and re-design the packet from scratch - every time he smiles he looks like a cracked cow-pat, every time he opens his mouth the neighbours reach for the double-glazing, every time he stops to think another hair falls out of his nose. Against which it should be said that very few people have the remotest idea who he is or what he looks like, so maybe we worry too much.

11) WOMEN

Apart from the PM we don't appear to have a single woman whose sex seems likely to be an asset to man or beast, and a number who have in the past proved serious liabilities (Knight J springs violently to mind). Viz not a lot of distaff Tories look as though they shop at Tesco's, have kids at Comprehensives, husbands on the dole etc; most in fact appear to spend their leisure at the hairdressers or abroad, and it shows (Oppenheim S is a prime example). Difficult to crack, this: but one of the simplest ways to bring a bit of humanity into the lives of these matrons is a Personal Tragedy (Mark T vanishes in desert, Mum weeps openly, Mary Whitehouse's 'We Stand By Our Son' and so on). Your department, I think, but let us know if we can help on the publicity side.

Otherwise all seems under control: look forward to hearing from you.

Regards,

Charles Saaaaaatchi'n'Saaaaaatchi

Mrs Thatcher shares a joke with Not the Nine O'clock News star Mel Smith.

6

Feb '83
Mrs T. acknowledges the boos of the crowd as she mounts the rostrum to receive her Nobel War Prize.

The Thatcher family watch in helpless horror as Mr Edward Heath and Sir Ian Gilmour are savagely assaulted by over-enthusiastic Young Conservatives at the 1982 Central Office Christmas party.

THE SAYINGS OF MRS THATCHER

● Of course Denis was my second love—I lost contact with my first love when he invaded Poland. (Interview with Godfrey Winn 1932)

● Our house was spotless. There was not a speck of dust anywhere. In my home we believed that cleanliness and 24 servants is next to Godliness. (On her childhood)

● I've no idea why people don't like me. (During her campaign to abolish education for the working classes)

● My greatest strength, I suppose, is that, come what may, there's always my Swiss bank account. (Panorama)

● The women of this country have never had a prime minister who knew the things they know . . . any woman who understands the problems of running a home will be nearer to understanding the problems of running a country. (On her bill to fit nuclear submarines with chintz curtains)

The Conservative and Unionist Party

June 9th

Messrs Saaaaaatchi'n'Saaaaaatchi

Dear Chas,

Thanks for your notes.

Briefly:

1) PM's shoes: the only person who's allowed anywhere near Margaret's feet is Ian Gow, who tells me he thinks it's chiefly a verruca problem, but will let us know more next time he sees them.

2) Willie was a bit upset by your remarks, and claims he dropped "jolly good" a couple of years ago in favour of "how are you? splendid etc". Is this OK?

3 & 4) see what we can do.

5) I've asked. Hobby: collecting wartime Nazi insignia. Favourite Room: a sort of bunker place underneath his garage equipped with the necessaries to cope with nuclear war, civil rising etc. Sensible enough in its own way, but not what we're looking for.

6) The halves date back to a bladder problem, but he thinks he's got one of those trick glasses somewhere which should do the trick. Pub-wise he'll fit in with whatever you come up with as long as he doesn't have to drink Watneys.

7) Michael takes the point, but has no objection to dressing up more often, and has gone ahead and ordered one of those cavalry lancer's uniforms with the plaited braid waistcoats and velvet capes, says he has a friend with a horse who's happy to help out when needed. I think you'd better talk to him direct about exactly what you had in mind: I'm a bit confused.

8 & 9) points taken.

10) I think you're right: we worry too much. A lot of people seem to confuse him with Eric Varley for some reason.

11) I'd rather talk this over face to face for obvious reasons, but the principle seems entirely sound. Ian Sproat has some friends with experience in this area, ex-SAS and so on. But we'd need to budget accordingly and hand the whole thing over to reliable sub-contractors, so to speak. Did you have a particular " tragedy " in mind? Which days are best for TV and newspaper coverage?

See you next week, & keep up the good work. M appreciates it greatly, and I'm sure will find ways of showing her gratitude come New Year.

Best wishes,

Cecil

7

WILL D

LABOUR

*JOBS

An immediate reduction in the number of unemployed by over 2 MILLION

Can't be done? Within 8 seconds of taking office, a Labour government would bring unemployment below the million mark by

RAISING the school-leaving age to 27

REDUCING the statutory retirement age to 31

CUTTING the working week to 7 hours

*TAXES

All politicians say they'll cut taxes. We **mean** it. Labour pledges to

ABOLISH the marginal tax rates on rape seed imports from Guyana

RAISE THRESHOLDS of pain for anyone currently living above the poverty line

REDISTRIBUTE the tax burden among the same people but rename the ways we do it

*DEFENCE

Labour is committed to abandoning **all** nuclear weapons as soon as we can devise an ecologically safe way of disposing of our existing stocks.

UNILATERALISM is vital to the NEC's bargaining position with the left wing of the party and potential CND voters—without it we cannot negotiate from a position of real strength. But of course we'd be happy as sandboys if we could get rid of unilateralism altogether

*EUROPE

Labour is committed to withdrawal from the EEC: see above

*INDUSTRY

Labour would make available up to **£5,000 billion** to manufacturing industry in the form of IOUs, Credit Cards and vague long-term promises

*SOCIAL SERVICES

Labour will work to get our **schools**, **hospitals** and **welfare services** back to the unholy mess they were in ten years ago, **starting now**

HOW'S ALL THIS GOING TO BE PAID FOR, MATE?

Of course Labour's plans will cost money: roughly £27,000 billion
But the money's there already
Here are some of the ways we'd raise the necessary revenues:

Sale of Commemorative Plaques and Postage Stamps	£2 million
Sale of US Military Secrets to Libya	£400 million
Not bothering to rescue Mark Thatcher	£1 million
Reducing number of courses at State Banquets to 23	£3 million
Libel actions against the "Daily Mail"	£6.5 million
Commercial Sponsorship of televised Parliamentary Debates	£17 million
Car Window Tax	£987 million
Extortion	£765 million
Levy on Homosexual Acts in Northern Ireland	£110 million
Profits from non-function of new-style phone boxes	£27.8 million
Mortgaging national assets	£10,000 billion
Printing bank notes	£14,680.7 billion
	£27,000 billion

ELIVER *

THE WILSON YEARS

1. The young Wilson canvassing, Liverpool 1926.
2. As the youngest Trade minister in Attlee's 1945 administration.
3. In retirement, Isles of Scilly, 1981.

Ebbw Vale! Labour's 16091 votes are taken out of storage.

Here it is—the first London bus to be fitted with a clock for short-sighted passengers.

"Let's hope it's the first of many" chirps a chirpy Ken Livingstone.

*UK mainland only

HISTORY OF THE LABOUR PARTY

44BC: Assassination of Julius Caesar
1381AD: Peasants' Revolt
1883: Death of Karl Marx
1887: Co-op Movement founded, Rochdale
1892: Co-op cut price of Family Firkin of Own Brand Dripping Mix to 1¾d
1894: 'A Friendly Society For The Provision of Toilet Paper In Jam Factories' founded, Merthyr Tydfil. Keir Hardie demands Universal Sufferage, cheaper dog licences, greater access to Society pages of 'Illustrated London News' and 'Boys Own Paper'; or else
1895: Hebden Bridge Pudding Riots
1897: Corinthian Casuals reach 4th round of FA Cup. Keir Hardie elected to Parliament, Harold Wilson not born yet
1900: First conference of the Independent Labour Party votes to expel itself from membership
1906: Inspired by the birth of Harold Wilson, ILP wins 29 Westminster seats. Michael Foot breaks leg
1914: In an attempt to divert attention from Harold Wilson's 8th Birthday celebrations, the Kaiser invades Belgium
1915: Wilson turns down seat in War Cabinet, volunteers for dangerous solo mission behind German lines which leads ultimately to collapse of German war effort, discovery of penicillin, invention of jazz
1918-62: Wilson lays down foundations of modern Labour Party as we know it
1963: Wilson elected Party leader
1964: Wilson becomes Prime Minister. Comets Fall From Sky, Blind Men See Again, Huge Vegetables Sprout From Ground All Over County Durham. Co-op stops giving cash divvy to customers
1965-9: Under Wilson's wise and benign guidance a Golden Age dawns. England win World Cup, Beatles appear on cover of 'Readers Digest', government pledges to provide a Mini-Cooper for every worker. Peter Tatchell born
1970: Tory Party, with joint Russian and Chinese backing, stages coup d'etat, takes over BBC, Watford Football Club, VIP cafeteria at Heathrow Airport. Wilson forced into exile in Scilly Islands, friends and supporters thrown into jail
1974: Nation rises as one man (J Gormley) overthrows Heath junta. Despite his dog's illness, Wilson is persuaded to return to office. But by now Enemies of the State have infiltrated many important Party posts
1976: Wilson resigns to make way for an older man. Death of the modern Labour Party as we know it.

copyright H Wilson 1983

9

THE AL

SDP

MEET THE SDP

LEADER•THE ECONOMY AND SO ON
Rt Hon Roy Jenkins MP

PRESIDENT•HOME AFFAIRS
The Equally Hon Shirley Williams MP

DEPUTY LEADER•FOREIGN AFFAIR
The Quite Hon David Owen MP

WE OPPOSE
* The Two-Party System
* The Present Unsatisfactory Way of Electing MPs
* The Amount of Money the Two Main Parties Have At Their Disposal
* A Lot of What They Both Stand For Anyway Regardless Of the Money Thing

WE RESENT
* The way we get treated in the House of Commons, particularly by bar staff and those whose responsibility it is to administer the issuing of car park passes and stationery requisitions

WE'VE HAD ABOUT AS MUCH AS WE CAN TAKE OF
* Roy Jenkins Claret Jokes
* Shirley Williams Hairdresser Jokes
* Snide references to Volvos and Habitat and The Guardian Woman's Page

FRANKLY IF THIS GOES ON MUCH LONGER
* Someone's going to get hurt

WE SUPPORT
* The Third World * The Arts Council * The National Trust
* Anything associated with the words Community, Leisure, Shared, Alternative, New, Improved, Help, Youth, Pluralistic, Ethnological, Radical Reassessment, Co-operative, Internationalist, Sugar-Free, Democratic, Self-Assembly, Latin American, Humanist, Futon, Devolved, Bicycle, Scandinavia

WE'D LIKE TO SEE
* The Police wear more casual uniforms
* Public Offices using only Charity Christmas Cards
* A nicer-smelling floor polish in hospitals
* Tax concessions to help West Indians buy more subdued furniture for their homes
* Cheaper classified advertising in the 'Sunday Times' and 'Observer'
* Universal Peace and Prosperity, Justice and Equality
* More women hooligans at football matches
* And a lot else besides, although sometimes we're not sure why we bother for all the support and help we get from the so-called caring, educated, politically aware classes who should know better, God knows

DISCOUNT SHOPPING Lord Harris

ALTERNATIVE CA PARKING Lord George Brown

FOREIGN TRAVEL, ENERGY, TECHNOLOGY, AEROBICS, ENG LI' Anthony Sampson M/

HEALTH AND BEAUTY, FURNITURE CARE, MEALS ON WHEEL INVISIBLE MENDIN DEFENCE, WALL COVERINGS Colin & Edna Baker, The Tre Berkhamsted, Herts

LIANCE

WHAT THE LIBERALS SAY...

"It's simple—you just put your lips together and suck"—Clement Freud MP

"I'm not saying my mother-in-law's Irish. In fact she's Pakistani!"—Cyril Smith MP

"But then she wouldn't, would she . . .?"—Alan Beith MP

"If you can't think of anything nice to say, then don't say anything at all!"—Bambi

"Policies? Policies? If there's one thing post war politics have taught us it's that policies don't work!"—Rt Hon David Steel MP

THE OTHER ONE
William Rodgers MP

)-OWNERSHIP,
ORK-SHARING
ck Taverne QC

CAR PARKING
Burlington Bertie from Bow

RST AID Michael
homas MP

ELECTORAL REFORM,
GARDEN FURNITURE
Bruce Douglas-Mann

CAL RADIO,
CHOOL
NIFORMS,
)LOUR OF BUSES
om McNally MP

HOW TO
ENTERTAIN
CHILDREN ON WET
WEEKENDS "Uncle Harry"

Clunk Click Every Trip. Yes, David Steele's hernia is much more serious than his colleagues imagined.

Cyril Smith MP worries out a morsel of lunch from his occipital cavity.

LIBERALS CARE ABOUT THE OLD VALUES

A 9th century law introduced by King Ethelred the Rotund which decreed that peasants must hand over half the contents of their pantry to their local MP (The Pantry Tax), is still strictly enforced in Rochdale, the constituency represented by Cyril Smith.

THE OTHER PARTIES

Our legal department spent many hours debating whether or not it was morally right to publish this picture. In the end it was decided that in all fairness it was our duty to do so. This is one of those thingies you see at the top of women's legs.

10 Least Sensible Political Parties involved in the election

1. Coast Erosion and Gulls Eggs Concern Party. (CEGECP)
2. Pontefract Cake Eaters Against the Bomb. (PCEAB)
3. Elvis is not Dead but only Resting White Residents Party. (EDRWRP)
4. Bring Back Hanging and National Service that'll Teach the Bastards Alliance. (BBHNSTBA)
5. Fish is not Meat Vegetarians Co-operative. (FNMVC)
6. Give Britain Back to Libya Movement. (GBBLM)
7. Stop Making Jokes About Dyna-Rod they're Doing a Good Job Cymru. (SMJADRDGJC)
8. Make Love Not Felt Hats Democratic Marxists. (MLNFHDM)
9. Unghhh Pom Pom Garden Dibblers and Coo Coo Nnggsshh Party (UPPGDCCNP)
10. The Social Democratic Party (SDP)

THE COMMUNIST PARTY OF GREAT BRITAIN (1983) LTD

The Manifesto

The Communist Manifesto (est. 1848) shows the only true path forward to a glorious future. A world where men and women with huge shiny biceps stride forward equally into a millenium of world peace, prosperity and happiness.

The Five Year Plan

The Five Year Plan sets out how this can be achieved

Stage One: Everyone's brain to be removed

Stage Two: Everyone to dress up in huge grey serge suits and furry hats, go to the nearest shop and start queueing

Stage Three: A forty per cent increase in the production of manganese nodules, tractor parts, beetroot, army boots, tin ore, string underpants, concrete rostrums, diodes, sulphuric acid, cordite, cabbage smells, barium sulphate, bollards, armoured cars and bathplugs.

Stage Four: More secret police. Electrodes fitted to everyone's genitals.

Stage Five: World peace, prosperity, happiness, huge shiny biceps etc.

THE NATIONAL GAY ALLIANCE PARTY

The National Gay Alliance Party stands for the principle that gay people are *exactly the same as everyone else* and should be treated as such) EXCEPT in the matters of:

— what we use our bottoms for
— what we use other people's bottoms for
— the fact that we prefer duller and more bottom-oriented television programmes
— the fact that we would prefer to see something a little different on Page Three of 'The Sun' — namely a bottom

What is it about a gay person that makes them different? Well, not much. The bottoms, of course. And a few other, tell-tale signs. We use soft loo paper. We like to drive black Porsche turbos. We prefer teaspoons to stir our coffee with, rather than the little white plastic twigs that so-called 'normal' people enjoy using. Otherwise, we're indistinguishable from anyone else: the same hopes and frustrations, the same needs and wants, the same willies and bottoms.

OUR POLICIES ARE:

* the abolition of the House of Lords, and its replacement by a House of Bottoms
* an immediate reduction in the number of private bottoms in the NHS
* government grants for the refurbishment of decaying inner-city bottoms
* nationalization of the 'Big Four' bottoms in the City of London
* training of young people to do skilled jobs: particularly where this involves rummaging around in bottoms
* helping the 'old folk' to get their trousers off
* all trade union members to be provided with a secret postal bottom before a strike
* a long, thoughtful look at the European Bottom Mountain
* American cruise bottoms on British soil to be fitted with a 'dual-key' system

The National Gay Alliance Party—we're right behind you

LOONY PARTIES
The Mayor of Merthyr Tydfil (r) seen enjoying a joke with the leader of Plaid Cymru, Mr Gwynfor Gwuyffyuddd.

The National Front Policy Committee in informal discussions with the Chairman of the National Gay Alliance Party

DEMOCRATIC RUTHLESS BASTARDS

If elected, the Democratic Ruthless Bastards pledge that they will:

* Introduce the death penalty for employees of Fast Food Restaurants who gob into the coleslaw
* Find out exactly who it is that sells the brown wee-wee that comes out of so-called 'coffee' machines and have the Sweeney break up their office until they emigrate
* Make taking the lift one floor only in a downwards direction punishable by a £500 fine
* Force people who let their dogs shit on the pavement to eat it all up with a spoon to teach them some manners
* Legalise armed robbery in all banks where they charge 50p to cash a cheque when it's not your branch
* Allow the parents of murdered children to execute the sods who did it in a manner of their choosing
* Create a new division of the police whose job it will be to stop any vehicle which is belching black smoke and shove the exhaust pipe*** up the driver's behind.

***or funnel

This partly black woman has been unemployed for over thirty years.

Labour's job creation scheme seen in action. First the people on the right interview the people on the left, then next day the people on the left interview the people on the right and so on and so forth until Friday when they all get huge salaries.

THE DEPRESSION RECESSION

Many visitors to our shores have shown surprise at the way Britain has changed after 4 years of Tory cuts. (P) Stratford-on-Avon tidies up for the tourist season.

THE

Argentine pilots rehearse the re-capture of the Malvinas

Men of Royal Greenjackets wade through Mrs Thatcher's crocodile tears in Port Stanley

THE FALKLANDS FACTORY

With hatred shining on her face, Mrs Thatcher plunges an SAS bayonet into a tin of Argentine corned beef.

DEFENCE

Ebbw Vale: The Rt Hon Michael Foot brandishes the Labour Party's answer to Russia's SS20's.

ISSUES

Mrs Thatcher combines security with style with new harmony bullet-proof hair lacquer.

LAW & ORDER

An official vehicle gives Toxteth's Conservative voter, Mrs. Elaine Nimmol, a lift to the polling station.

Police demonstrate the new regulations which require them to knock on a car door before shooting the occupants.

15

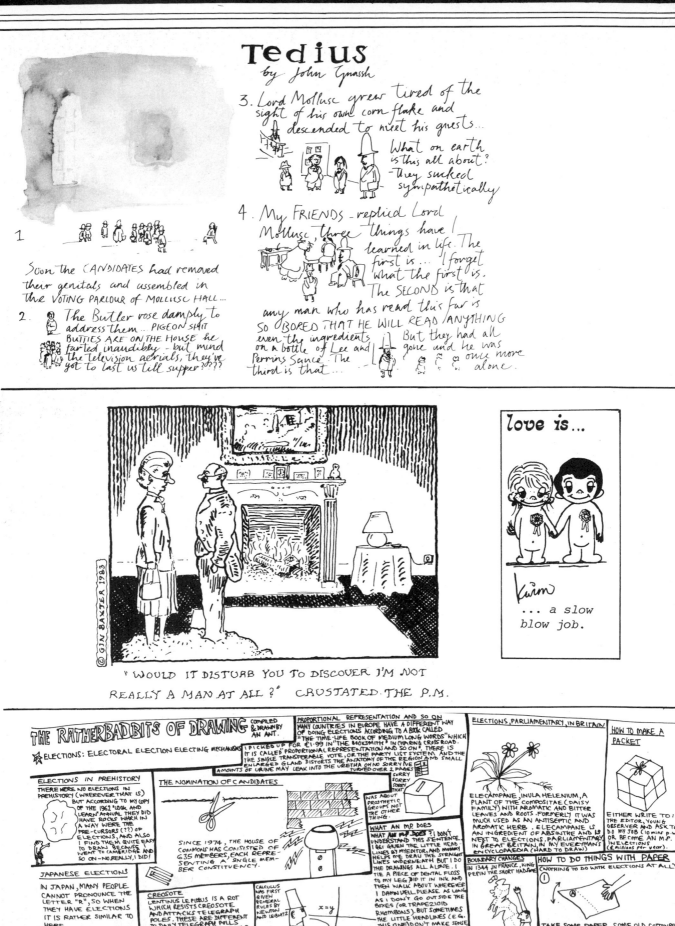

Tedius
by John Gnash

3. Lord Mollusc grew tired of the sight of his own corn flake and descended to meet his guests...

What on earth is this all about? —They sucked sympathetically

1

Soon the CANDIDATES had removed their genitals and assembled in the VOTING PARLOUR OF MOLLUSC HALL...

2 The Butler rose damply to address them... PIGEON SHIT BUTTIES ARE ON THE HOUSE he farted inaudibly — but mind the television aerials, they've got to last us till supper?º???

4. My FRIENDS —replied Lord Mollusc, three things have I learned in life. The first is... I forget what the first is. The SECOND is that any man who has read this far is SO BORED THAT HE WILL READ ANYTHING even the ingredients on a bottle of Lee and Perrins Sauce. The third is that... But they had all gone and he was once more alone.

© GIN BAXTER 1983

" WOULD IT DISTURB YOU TO DISCOVER I'M NOT REALLY A MAN AT ALL ?" CRUSTATED. THE P.M.

love is...

Kim

... a slow blow job.

THE RATHERBADBITS OF DRAWING
COMPILED & DRAWN BY AN ANT.

ELECTIONS: ELECTORAL ELECTION ELECTING MECHANISMS

PROPORTIONAL REPRESENTATION AND SO ON MANY COUNTRIES IN EUROPE HAVE A DIFFERENT WAY OF DOING ELECTIONS ACCORDING TO A BOOK CALLED "THE TIME-LIFE BOOK OF MEDIUM LONG WORDS" WHICH I PICKED UP FOR £1·99 IN "THE BOOKSMITH" IN CHARING CROSS ROAD. IT IS CALLED PROPORTIONAL REPRESENTATION AND SO ON. THERE IS THE SINGLE TRANSFERABLE VOTE, OR THE PARTY LIST SYSTEM AND THE ENLARGED GLAND DISTORTS THE ANATOMY OF THE REGION AND SMALL AMOUNTS OF URINE MAY LEAK INTO THE URETHA OH NO SORRY IVE TURNED OVER 2 PAGES

WAS ABOUT SORRY SORRY SORRY THAT WAS ABOUT PROSTHETIC GROUPS NOT THE OTHER THING.

ELECTIONS, PARLIAMENTARY, IN BRITAIN

ELECAMPANE, INULA HELENIUM, A PLANT OF THE COMPOSITAE (DAISY FAMILY) WITH AROMATIC AND BITTER LEAVES AND ROOTS. FORMERLY IT WAS MUCH USED AS AN ANTISEPTIC AND AROMATIC HERB. ELECAMPANE IS AN INGREDIENT OF ABSINTHE AND IS NEXT TO ELECTIONS, PARLIAMENTARY IN GREAT BRITAIN, IN MY EVERYMAN'S ENCYCLOPAEDIA (HARD TO DRAW)

HOW TO MAKE A PACKET

EITHER WRITE TO: THE EDITOR, YOUNG OBSERVER AND ASK TO DO MY JOB (10 mins p.w.) OR, BECOME AN M.P. IN ELECTIONS (£ millions per year).

ELECTIONS IN PREHISTORY
THERE WERE NO ELECTIONS IN PREHISTORY (WHEREVER THAT IS) BUT ACCORDING TO MY COPY OF THE 1962 "LOOK AND LEARN" ANNUAL THEY DID HAVE ROCKS WHICH IN A WAY WERE THE PRE-CURSORS (??) OF ELECTIONS, AND ALSO I FIND THEM QUITE EASY TO DRAW BECAUSE I WENT TO CAMBRIDGE AND SO ON - NO REALLY, I DID!

THE NOMINATION OF CANDIDATES
SINCE 1974, THE HOUSE OF COMMONS HAS CONSISTED OF 635 MEMBERS, EACH REPRE-SENTING A SINGLE MEM-BER CONSTITUENCY.

WHAT AN MP DOES
WHAT AN MP DOES? I DON'T UNDERSTAND THIS SENTENCE. I BEG GIVEN THE LITTLE HEAD LINES BY MYEDITOR, AND MUMMY HELPS ME DRAW THE STRAIGHT LINES UNDERNEATH BUT I DO TIE A PIECE OF DENTAL FLOSS TO THE DRAWINGS ALL A LINE I I TIE A PIECE OF DENTAL FLOSS I DID IT IN INK AND THEN WALK ABOUT WHEREVER I DAMN WELL PLEASE, AS LONG AS I DON'T GO OUTSIDE THE BOXES (OR TRAPEZOID RHOMBONS), BUT SOMETIMES THE LITTLE HEADLINES (E.G. THIS ONE) DON'T MAKE SENSE WHAT AN MP DOES? AS FAR AS I KNOW DOES ARE THE FEMALE PLURAL OF DEER (OR MEMBERS OF THE FAMILY CERVIDAE IN THE SUBORDER RUMINANTIA OF THE ORDER ARTIODACTYLA) SO I HAVE PUT IN MY DRAWING FROM "THE INVENTION OR CALCULUS" & HOPE THE EDITOR DOESN'T NOTICE

JAPANESE ELECTIONS
IN JAPAN, MANY PEOPLE CANNOT PRONOUNCE THE LETTER "R", SO WHEN THEY HAVE ELECTIONS IT IS RATHER SIMILAR TO HERE.

TREMENDOUS STUDIES IN INDUSTRY

AN ENGLISH M.P. SPEAKING

CREOSOTE
LENTINUS LEPIDUS IS A ROT WHICH RESISTS CREOSOTE AND ATTACKS TELEGRAPH POLES. THESE ARE DIFFERENT TO DAILY TELEGRAPH POLLS WHICH OFTEN HAPPEN NEAR ELECTIONS.

CALCULUS WAS FIRST GIVEN GENERAL RULES BY NEWTON AND LEIBNITZ.

x = y

BOUNDARY CHANGES
IN 1344 IN FRANCE, KING PEPIN THE SHORT HAD ...

HOW TO DO THINGS WITH PAPER
(NOTHING TO DO WITH ELECTIONS AT ALL)

①

TAKE SOME PAPER, SOME OLD COTTON REELS, SOME EXTRACT OF CARBORUNDUM, A PAPER CLIP, ESSENCE OF CARPENTERS SCUD-OIL, AND A PAIR OF SCISSORS. THROW EVERYTHING AWAY EXCEPT THE PAPER: YOU WILL NOW BE ABLE TO DO THINGS WITH IT.

CANVASSING

SDP candidate Julian Fanshaw has a novel way of attracting crowds to hear him speak—he hangs dogs.

Unfair, dirty and immoral campaigning are just some of the allegations thrown at Norman St John Stevas seen here touring his constituency of Chelmsford.

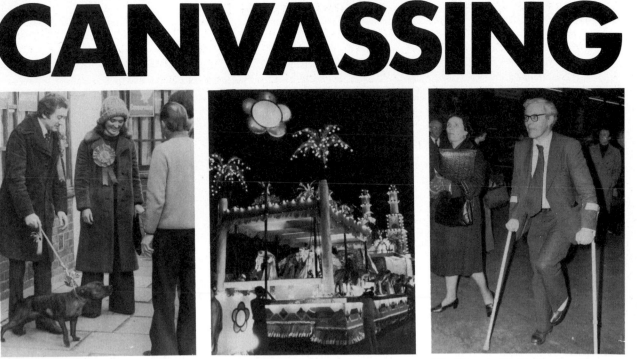

The 'Sympathy Vote'. An old political ploy—pretending that you want to pee but there's no one to get it out and hold it for you. Usually worth a few votes.

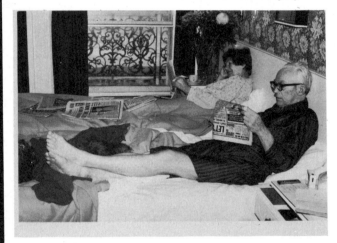

A couple of political intellectuals frolic indulgently in a bout of sexual foreplay.

An anxious Mrs Thatcher discovers that there aren't enough public conveniences in her Finchley constituency.

This picture shows a candidate canvassing two voters. There are five reasons in the photograph why he will not get their votes—can you spot them?
(Answers at foot of page 19)

UNDER CANVAS

The precise origin and function of canvassing remain one of the great unsolved mysteries of 20th Century behaviourism. There is no evidence to suggest that the ritual is in any way beneficial to either canvasser or canvassed—in fact such evidence as there is strongly suggests that the process is entirely counter-productive. So why does it survive? Dunmore and Hook, in their workmanlike monogramme "The Use of Elections in the Treatment of NSU and Halitosis" (Belgrade, 1922) suggest undertones of psychotic fantasy: that the nervous approach of the canvasser to the stranger's front door is the preliminary to a potentially painful anal insertion. Hard to know what to make of that, really (the same authors, of course, have in the past suggested that it is possible to gather accurate information about male genitalia from studying a man's socks; and that Rhodes Boyson's reluctance to shave the sides of his face stems from an adolescent desire to be beaten with a lavatory brush).

More recent research has focussed on finding out what canvassers would be doing with their time if they weren't canvassing. The results of a 1979 survey among canvassers from all the major parties indicate that a majority (53%) would have been talking to someone, but only a tiny minority (0.3%) would have been listening to what the other person had to say. Of the remainder, 17% would have been queueing in a Post Office; 14% writing letters to Any Answers, 6% watching their lives drift by and wishing they'd gone to live in South Africa after the war, 2% drinking Mellow Birds with a neighbour, and the others either grooming a pet or working. Conservatives put canvassing below gardening but above sex in their choice of leisure activities; among Labour Party workers it was looked on as a welcome excuse to escape from the realities of their own lives.

Answers:
1. Both ladies are deaf, and think he is the gas man.
2. He has arrived just as they are sitting down to their only hot meal of the week. Although they're too polite to say anything, their minds are not on politics.
3. Both are Belgian nationals.
4. Their mothers told them never to trust a man who fondles the contents of his pocket in mixed company.
5. The candidate is a member of the Labour Party.

UNDERSTAND YOUR MP

During the run up to the election you are almost certain to have at least one politician knocking on your door to say "Hello". But what does "Hello" really mean?

Here is a brief phrasebook to help you . . .

Hello	I've ignored you for 5 years but now I'm here again.
How are you?	Please don't tell me, I haven't the slightest interest in your health, only your vote.
What a cute little baby!	Ugh. It has snot coming out of its *ears*!
Can I count on your vote?	You look like a stupid person.
Our party is the party for you.	Our party is the party for me.
If I'm elected I promise I will look into it for you.	The minute our conversation is ended I will have completely forgotten that you exist.
We are going through a world recession	Our policies were a disaster and we made a balls of everything.
We'll fight unemployment	We are going through a world recession.
I represent the ( ) party.	Can't you see my rosette you blind twat?
I agree with you.	I need your vote so I would be a twit to disagree with you.
I can sympathise because my mother is a pensioner too.	And my father owns a chain of supermarkets.
I strongly believe . . .	I've never really thought about it. . .
That's a very good question.	I wish you hadn't asked me that.
No matter where your sympathies lie it is your duty to vote.	If you're not voting for me then for God's sake stay away from the polling station.
Just because I'm a Tory doesn't mean I agree with everything that Mrs Thatcher says.	All Hail the Blessed Margaret, Earthly Goddess, Mistress of my soul and my destiny.
Just because I'm a Socialist doesn't mean I'm a Communist.	. . . we'll keep the Red flag flying here . . .
Just because I'm a Liberal doesn't mean I'm a crank.	Not only will we make paedophilia legal but we'll make it compulsory.
Blibble flump guggle guggle pobbly pob.	Just because I'm a Social Democrat doesn't mean I talk a load of rubbish.
It's been very nice talking to you but I really must dash along.	You're obviously going to vote for me so there's no point me wasting time on you.
Look forward to seeing you again soon.	Look forward to you moving so I won't have to see you in five years' time.

YOUR NEW BOUNDARIES: LET ME EXPLAIN.

WHAT'S HAPPENING, EXACTLY?

Since the last General Election, the Boundary Commission has implemented a number of minor adjustments in the size and number of Parliamentary Constituencies. This is a routine procedure, regularly undertaken in all democracies in order to rationalise the electorate (such administrative adjustments are common on the continent, as for example in Russia in 1917, in Germany in 1933, in Spain in 1936; and an almost daily occurrence in Albania and Haiti*).

I SEE. SO WHAT'S HAPPENING, EXACTLY?

Up to now, we've had over **six hundred** individual constituencies, scattered round the country, each with its own electorate, party organisations, returning officer and so on. Under the new plan things will be much simpler.
All the traditional Labour seats have been amalgamated into two new centralised constituencies, each with its own Member of Parliament. Those areas which have in the past elected Liberal, SDP or other minority representatives have been brought together to form a single voting unit, which will have **its** Member, too. The remaining 29 Members will be . . .

HOLD ON A MINUTE . . .

Don't interrupt. The remaining 29 Members will be shared by the Conservative electorate. It's as easy as that.

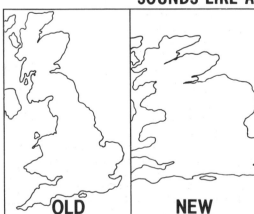

OLD   NEW

DOES THIS MEAN THAT I'LL NEED A NEW TELEVISION AERIAL?

Not necessarily.

THAT'S A RELIEF!

With a few exceptions** it has not proved economic to physically move people's residences from one constituency to another. Normally, you will be able to continue living in your existing home, but will be issued with a new address and postcode. For example people living in that part of the London Borough of Brent which lies between Finchley Road and the North Circular have been transferred for administrative purposes to the outskirts of Ullapool. And so on.

SOUNDS LIKE A GREAT IDEA! BUT WHAT'S ALL THIS GOING TO COST?

Less than you think***. In fact in a lot of ways it could even end up **saving** us**** money.

ANOTHER CUP OF TEA, MRS T?

I'd love one. Just hold on while I find a photographer.

*Ah, but we didn't say **which** continent, did we?

**Jews, Gypsies and Darkies. The Irish'll have to wait for next time round.
***i.e. less than we'd like to think you think.
****But not you.

THE 23RD BITSANPISI BRITISH GENERAL ELECTION

in association with HRH Queen Elizabeth II

ON THE DAY

32 page pull-out

SPECIAL COLOUR SUPPLEMENT

13 Minicab cards.
1 notification of Bank Holiday refuse collection arrangements.
1 Free Newspaper full of double glazing ads.
16 Photo processing envelopes.
1 Postcard from New Zealand intended for a total stranger living at your address.
3 Rubber Bands.

****You are not insane.** If you are insane, you may **not** know by now. An easy test of your sanity is to attempt to work out whether people like Selina Scott because she looks like Princess Di, or vice versa.
****You are not Royal.** If you are Royal and do not know it, you may already be disqualified (see above).
****You are not in prison.** If you are hoping to go to prison but are still on a waiting list, you might be better off shopping around for an overseas prison, or getting yourself locked up privately. In the meantime, you are allowed to vote if you must.

WHO CAN VOTE?

Anyone born before October 1975 is legally entitled to vote, provided that:
****You are registered.** If you are on the electoral roll, you should know by now. Registered voters automatically get through their letterbox a free Citizens Factpack containing:
31 out-of-date detergent discount vouchers.
1 Residents Association Jumble Sale notice.

HOW TO VOTE – A GUIDE TO FIRST-TIME VOTERS

Spoiled ballot papers are a nuisance. They make a mockery of our democratic constitution, they are unproductive and they are a constant source of irritation to political candidates. Follow these simple instructions on the correct way to vote . . . and make your vote count.

At the polling station you will be given a slip of paper like this

SMITH	
JONES	
BROWN	
DANDINI AND HIS DISAPPEARING DOVES	
CILLYTHWAT	

First of all, draw a line through the name of any candidates you feel are likely to crap on your head if elected

SMITH	
JONES	
BROWN	
~~DANDINI AND HIS DISAPPEARING DOVES~~	
CILLYTHWAT	

Now make your selection and draw a cat's face in the square provided

SMITH	
JONES	
BROWN	
DANDINI AND HIS DISAPPEARING DOVES	
CILLYTHWAT	🐱

In each of the remaining squares draw a fish

SMITH	🐟
JONES	🐟
BROWN	🐟
DANDINI AND HIS DISAPPEARING DOVES	🐟
CILLYTHWAT	🐱

Finally, and because your vote is a secret, tear off your selection and hide it in your pocket

SMITH	🐟
JONES	🐟
BROWN	🐟
DANDINI AND HIS DISAPPEARING DOVES	🐟

REMEMBER—IT IS YOUR DUTY TO VOTE.

6.30 Good Morning Viewer (TV am)
7.0 Breakfast Time Election Special
Frank and Selina take a topical look at the world of politics with some timely tips on what to wear to the polls, some tasty declaration snacks, and an inspired guess at what the night ahead has in store for Russell Grant.
10.0 Schools Broadcasting (BBC 1)
Very simple sums for sixth formers, followed by first steps in spelling for school leavers.

Arthur Askey (Afternoon Cinema, Channel 4)

Call My Bluff (BBC 2, 8.30). Who or what is an Sdpsdpsdpsdps—a mediaeval publisher's plug? A town in Poland? an Intestinal infection?

Veteran actors Terry and Percy Rudders play the two halves of William Whitelaw's bottom in Granada's reconstruction of The Lord Mayor's Banquet (ITV, 7.30)

Lord Hailsham demonstrates how to cover up an unexpected trouser stain (Home Care, Channel 4, 4.45)

THE RIVALS

ITV	BBC
* Alastair Burnet	* David Dimbleby
* Robert Kee	* Robin Day
* Trevor MacDonald	* David Butler
* A Computer Called DORIS	* A Computer called TULIP
* Only one man who understands how it works	* No-one who understands how it works
* A Blackboard	* A Blackboard
* A lot of young ladies in t-shirts and jogging suits running around with bits of paper	* A lot of ladies who look as though life is passing them by sitting round staring into the middle distance
* A black lesbian weather forecaster	* Richard Stilgoe with a song about the weather
* Edward du Cann	* Jo Grimond

11.45 Moomins in Voterland (ITV)
1.07 Commercial Break (Channel 4)

Richard Clayderman isn't just an ordinary pianist: he's a very ordinary pianist. But thousands of Frenchwomen suspect he may have an enormous banana in his pocket. This banana is **not** available through the post, but a picture of it is on the cover of the cassette box. Send money now before it turns brown and mushy.

7.0 The Youngish Ones (BBC 1)

The zany pranksters are confused when Alexei Sayle turns up on the doorstep without his script. (Rpt)

7.30 The Election Alternative (Channel 4)

Why do women still only get one vote? Why can't Roumanians vote in British Elections? Where is Glasgow?

8.30 Who's Wife Are You Anyway? (BBC 2)

The fly-on-the-wall series catches up with a group of breakfasting Tory MPs in their hotel bedrooms during the Party Conference.

9.0 TV Torython (ITV)

In aid of the Monetarists In Need Appeal: this year the target is to lose a million jobs nationwide. Whether you're thinking of laying off a whole town, or simply think there might be an old family retainer in the attic you don't need any more, every job counts. And if the phones stop ringing a host of elderly Variety Club artistes will come on and do their turns until they start again.

Anthony Andrews is Dr Heseltine in "The Herpes Syndrome" (BBC 2 11.50)

**Dan Archer
Radio 4. 6.45 pm**

5.45 a.m. Farmers' Fiddle (Radio 4)

Arthur Stubb goes down Cheltenham way to have breakfast with a couple who haven't paid a penny's tax in fifty years, own three Range Rovers, sent their sons to Harrow but still reckon farmers get a rough deal.

5.59 Gael Warning and Election Weather Special (Radio 4)

UHF only. Listeners on Long Wave get something that sounds like a fat frog being pulled through the neck of a thin bottle. Or perhaps it's two mating tortoises caught at just the moment they're interrupted by the telephone ringing. Hard to tell.

7.0 What Election! (Radio 1)

Mike Read opens up Radio 1's coverage by reading out researcher's questions to a trendy young don from Soho Poly and rephrasing the answers in monosyllables that assume his audience have an average age of eleven. Later Simon Bates comes on and sniggers a bit, he and Mike make a joke about **either** BBC tea **or** Dave Lee Travis's parking, then DLT and Peter Powell drop in to the studio and there are more giggles and plugs, Simon says something about Steve Wright's trousers which unfortunately none of us can see, then tells us he didn't mean it. Dave Jensen asks Brian Curtois to explain exactly what elections are, and why we have them. Plus Bucks Fizz, Lulu, Mark Almond. Participants get three points for sounding concerned about unemployment, but no points for getting angry about it.

7.0 Today Election Special (Radio 4)

Brian Redhead and John Timpson discuss how little there is to say until the results come in with Arthur Scargill, the weather man, Edward du Cann, a class of primary school children in South Shields, Gerald Priestland, the switchboard operator at Station KNOPQ Kansas City, and each other.

8.30 Election Morning Concert (Radio 3)

Mozart: Concerto for Gramophone Y Disci Egtonia.

9.0 News (IRN)

With phone quotes from John Carlisle, Garret FitzGerald, Willie Hamilton, Sir Freddie Laker, Ian Botham, the commissionaire at Station KNOPQ Kansas City, Lord George Brown.

9.10 Midweek (Radio 4)

Henry Kelly, Gloria Hunniford, Terry Wogan, Eamonn Andrews and John Cole talk about why there are so many programmes on radio and TV devoted to discussing why there are so many Irish men and women in British broadcasting.

10.30 Us and Ours (Radio 4)

The election issues as they affect middle class housewives in the Home Counties, with a special feature on what to do if you suspect your milkman of voting Labour.

11.0 Election Phone-In (ILR Stations)

Vyvyan White in the studio, taking calls from Willie Hamilton, John Carlisle, The Bishop of Birmingham, Lord George Brown, Garret FitzGerald, Sir Freddie Laker.

12.0 Hoots! (Radio 2)

Ludovic Kennedy is joined by Magnus Magnusson, Donald MacCormack, Stanley Baxter, Billy Connolly, Ronnie Corbett and others in a debate over why there are so few programmes on radio and television about how many Scots there are in broadcasting. (Not Wales)

12.30 I'm Sorry, It's Us Again! (Radio 4)

Team captains Frank Norden and Dennis Muir, helped out by Willy Rushton, Tim Brooke-Taylor, Kenneth Williams, Benny Green and a woman, in a special Election-day edition of the long-running pun-show.

2.30 The Count At Monte Cristo (Radio 4)

Afternoon Theatre in election mood. In 1812 the poet Byron nearly visits an Italian village where the selection of a parish priest goes ahead despite a slight south-easterly breeze. With the unmistakeable voices of the BBC Repertory Company.

5.0 Poll's Apart! (IRN)

Phone updates from around the country. Gavin Turp finds not much happening in rural East Anglia, Andrea Sprunt shouts at a school leaver in Toxteth, Laurie Understayne has a novelty piece about a polling booth in a public lavatory in Taunton.

6.30 Midweek (Radio 4)

Repeat of this morning's broadcast with the swear word taken out.

6.48 Shouting By Radio (World Service)

Frank Muir is back in "I'm Sorry, It's Us Again!"(Radio 4, 12.30)

8.30 Thirst Past The Post (Radio 4)

Derek Cooper finds an election pretext to savour some Australian brandies, an unusual cheesecake from South Korea, and an enormous dinner for one at Chez Plumpi's.

9.15 Capital Debate (Capital Radio)

With Willie Hamilton, Lord George Brown, The Bishop of Birmingham and Hercules the Bear.

10.0 Night and Hobday (Radio 2 with Radio 4)

Peter Hobday and friends take us through the night with a mixture of results, analysis and country music. Tonight's special election guest: Pete Murray.

ON THE DAY

At a glance!

WIN A TRIP TO FIJI
ELECTION NIGHT BALLOT BINGO

AMPLE-UNDER-LYME	BORROCKS	MID-CARDIGAN	RUNCIE
DRABBLE	BIRMINGHAM ACCENT	BEDWETTY	MANCHESTER WHITELAW
IRKUTSK NORTH	DARKIE	SPIRRAL	BARKER-WITH-CORBETT

Check off your bingo constituency as soon as they declare. When your card is full, take it **at once** and **in person** to the address below to claim your prize. Each Ballot Bingo Card is unique—all have been individually printed on different pieces of paper and distributed with different copies of this book. Winners should take their cards for verification to Department NTGE, The Cassava House, FIJI—Personal callers only.

=== ELECTION SEVEN ===

GOING: SOGGY

1 121 Conservative (97) Parkinson...M. Thatcher
2 212 Labour (65) Mortimer..............Various
3 000 Alliance (3) Steel.................R. Jenkins
4 000 Plaid Cymru (11) Evans...........G. Evans
5 000 Scot Nat (9) Sillers.................G. Wilson
6 000 Ulster Unionist (27) Paisley.J. Molyneaux
7 000 Sinn Fein (48) Adams...........O. Carron

ODDS: Con win 11/10. Lab win 6/7. Alliance win 2,500/1. Plaid claiming to have won Evens. Scot Nat remembering to turn up 50/1. Ulster Unionists offering to help a woman wash up 8,500/1. Sinn Fein accepting such an offer if made 8,501/1. Con doing what they've been promising they'd do next time 765,000/1. Roy Jenkins chances of getting back into the Labour Party 600,00/7. Chances of the government getting rid of the Falklands now the elections over Evens. Others: Arsenal to qualify for the Milk Cup 88/1. Chances of an MP having seen a TV programme he's complaining about 100/1. Chances of a nuclear war by the end of this week 2/1.

I SPY! ON ELECTION DAY:

A RETURNING OFFICER GOING INTO A BETTING OFFICE	4 PTS
AN ITV REPORTER INTERVIEWING A POLITICIAN ON BBC TV	5 PTS
ENOCH POWELL WEARING A T-SHIRT	25 PTS
TWO CANDIDATES' WIVES SMILING AT EACH OTHER	11 PTS
A MINISTER'S BODYGUARD WHO WISHES TO RELIEVE HIMSELF BUT IS ON DUTY	30 PTS
ROBIN DAY EATING	2 PTS

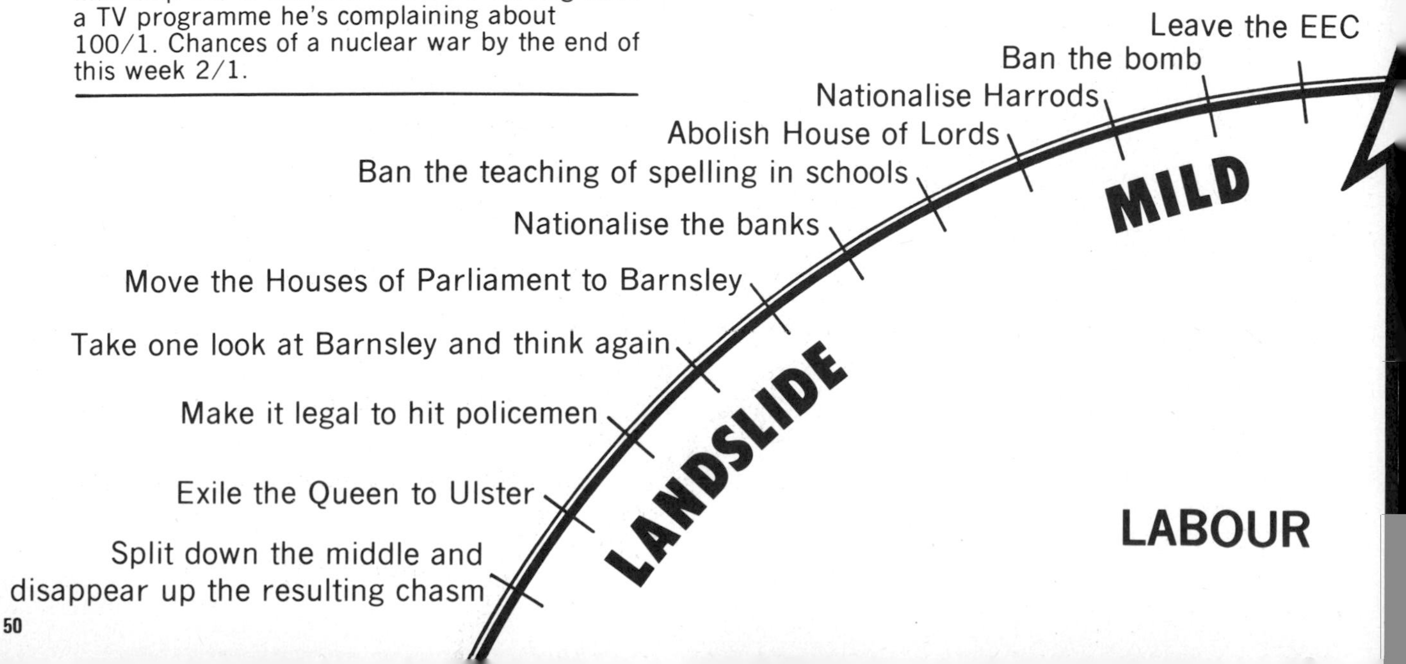

Leave the EEC
Ban the bomb
Nationalise Harrods
Abolish House of Lords
Ban the teaching of spelling in schools
Nationalise the banks
Move the Houses of Parliament to Barnsley
Take one look at Barnsley and think again
Make it legal to hit policemen
Exile the Queen to Ulster
Split down the middle and disappear up the resulting chasm

MILD

LANDSLIDE

LABOUR

THE PARTY MANIFESTOS AT A GLANCE

Tories will:

Fight inflation by controlling the money supply

Improve industrial output by increasing unemployment

Prop up unsuccessful new industries

Prop up fascist dictatorships in the Third World

Do sod all about Ulster

Pay for union ballots before a strike starts

Promote research into urban problems

Pretend to discourage immigration

Give in to the miners next time round

Build nuclear power-stations

Retain nuclear weapons

Retain public schools

Help the old folk cross the road

Press for vast new powers for the police

Press for vast new powers for the unions*

Look carefully at our membership of the EEC

Go on in the usual way about death penalty, social security scroungers, vandalism, pornography etc

*Poland only. Offer closes April 1984.

Labour will:

Fight inflation by building more schools and hospitals

Improve unemployment by increasing industrial output

Prop up unsuccessful old industries

Prop up Marxist dictatorships in the Third World

Do sod all about Ulster

Pay for union ballots before a strike ends

Promote research into urban problems

Pretend to encourage immigration

Give in to the miners next time round

Build coal-fired power-stations

Get rid of nuclear weapons

Abolish public schools

Help the old folk get jobs in the cabinet

Press for vast new powers for the unions

Press for vast new powers for anyone who hasn't already got some

Look carefully at our membership of NATO

Go on in usual way about House of Lords, grammar schools, nurses, media bias etc

Alliance will:

Fight inflation by radical new policies, fresh look at problem etc

Don't know

Prop up successful new wine bars

Press for proportional representation in the Third World

Eat more brown bread, regular exercise, fresh vegetables etc

A bit of both, really

Promote research into the problems of research into urban problems

Pretend not to notice what colour black people are at parties

Give in to the miners next time round

Lots of thick socks, thermal vests etc

Organise Women for Peace demos outside empty nissen huts in the hope that the Russians will assume they contain nuclear weapons

Retain public conveniences

Help the old folk, what's our policy on the old folk?

Press for vast new powers for the SDP

Press for vast new powers for gays, cripples, people with orange beards and pebble glasses, the bald, women who wear boiler-suits and shout a lot, people who can't pee while they're being watched, and plump middle-aged gentlemen who can't pronounce their "r"s properly

Look carefully at idea of offering free membership of EEC and NATO to all Barclaycard Owners

A bit of both, really

Sell off Wales

Abolish trade unions

Privatise the armed forces

Hand over the BBC to the Daily Mail

Replace the MCC selectors

Tax extra-marital sex

Force Prince Andrew to marry Carol Thatcher

Re-site the Treasury in The Cayman Islands

Bring in suitable penalties for sickness

Sell off the immigrant population

Invade Poland

MILD

LANDSLIDE

TORIES

ON THE DAY

CONSTITUENCIES TO WATCH OUT FOR

KEIGHLEY
(Lab maj 78)
A poor showing by Plaid Cymru here could provide a pointer to the Welsh Nationalist vote elsewhere in Yorkshire.

FINCHLEY
(Tory maj 7,878)
Always a popular declaration among gay viewers because of the opportunity it provides to examine the pride of the special Branch parading behind the Prime Minister.

GREENHAM COMMON
(Tory maj 13,081)
There have been considerable population changes at Greenham since 1979, most notably the addition of over half a million CND postal voters from Japan who are likely, along with 20,000 temporary Cuban residents, to favour the opposition parties; against which the Conservatives expect great things from a small Executive Housing development on the outskirts of Beenham village. Counting is expected to take around seven weeks.

HILLHEAD
(SDP maj 4,320)
Eight of the nine candidates have changed their names by deed poll to Roy Jenkins; the ninth, Mr Jenkins himself, has countered by changing *his* name to Brian Boru McFaddyen of That Ilk (1981) Ltd. All nine parties carry the initials SDP. There is speculation that McFaddyen's tactics in dissociating himself from the name Jenkins may work to his advantage.

LLANPITLY AND TRYFFID
(Lab maj 56,213)
The failure of the Constituency Labour Party to reselect Sir Evan Gwilwyn-Evans, who has held the seat unopposed since 1906, means that there are six Labour candidates, representing Labour, Official Labour, Independent Labour, Real Independent Labour, The Original Labour Party We Grew Up In (Social Democrat) and The Original Labour Party We Grew Up In (Marxist/Leninist). All six are members of Sir Evan's family, including three of his ex-wives and his lurcher.

BRIGHTON MARINA
A new constituency, made up of overspill from the old electorates of Hove Central and Ostend Maritime. The Gaullists are expected to make a strong showing against a coalition of Kent Apple-growers and People Who Can't Stand Yachtsmen In General And The Sort Of Yachtsmen You Find In Brighton In Particular.

BOURNEMOUTH CENTRAL
(Tory maj 675,976)
Another vote where a local issue may obscure the national pattern: the decision by the City Council to draw and quarter an Argentinian national found on a bus during the Falklands War, against the wishes of the sitting Member who favoured baking him in a pie and sending him to Sir Victor Matthews as a token of thanks for the contribution made by Max Hastings to the British victory. Also worth watching for a glimpse of the Returning Officer's dentures, which have been worn by all his predecessors in office since 1756.

BELFAST CAR-PARK
(OUOPNIUP maj 7)
A city centre seat whose electorate has shrunk in recent years to 27, being contested by a total of 68 parties (11 Protestant, 13 Catholic, 3 Mostly Protestant But We Don't Say So, 2 Mainly Catholic Ditto, 3 Non-Sectarian But Not Exactly Working Class Orientated, 1 Divine Light, 1 George Davis Is Innocent, 2 PLO, 1 Anorak and Balaclava Retailers Alliance, 1 Malvinas Action Group, 2 Levellers, 3 Corn Law Repealers, 2 Jacobite, 1 ZIPRA, 1 Van Morrison Fan Club, 6 Triads For A Faster Take-Away, 1 Policeman's Ball Fund.

LUNATICS TO WATCH OUT FOR

If you see one of these attempting to vote, stop him.

Three escaped lunatics attempt to vote illegally at a polling station in Liverpool by turning up disguised as Pamela Stephenson.

ELECTION Quiz

HUNDREDS OF PRIVATE MEMBERS BILLS TO BE WON!

1 What is Sir William Van Straubenzee's real name?

2 What is the correct way for a Member of Parliament to convey to the Speaker the fact that he wishes to go to the toilet during a debate?

3 Which one of the following has Sir Robin Day never referred to as "a possible future Prime Minister"?

Syd Little   Sarah Hogg
Vidal Sassoon   Buster Mottram
Douglas Adams   Francis Wilson
The Amazing Whelko   Michael Foot

4 What is the largest number of jokes about Shirley Williams' hair ever included in a single edition of "Week Ending": 11, 13 or 197?

5 How many expletives can you make by rearranging the letters in the name 'Saatchi and Saatchi'?

6 Who earns most: The Chairman of IBM, the King of Oman, or an MEP?

7 What **is** an MEP? What does he or she **do**, exactly?

8 Who gives a toss?

9 Why are the following so called:
Early Day Motions   Black Rod
Parliamentary Recesses   Private Members
Junior Whips   Lady Fuchs?

10 Study the picture. A wax figure has been introduced into the photograph (it's the one seated on the left, wearing the cheap imitation wedding ring). Using your skill and judgment try and estimate the time it would take Mr Whitelaw's right hand to reach Sir Geoffrey Howe's left buttock.

Send your answers, together with eight unused ballot papers, to: The Personation Officer, The Ulster Politicians Benevolent Society, PO Box H20, Magherafelt, N.I.

Hidden in the grid are the nicknames of the MPs whose pictures appear below. How many can you find and match? What are their real names?

```
T A D P O L E F A P P S L U G S
A I I U Q U E E N I E I T B F O
R A N D Y S G E N G H I S U U G
Z O G Y E T I L I L L E T S N G
A L L L A E U E Y E X F A N G Y
N A E O D R G R O T T E R T U T
C N D R O O P Y D R A W E R S O
X U A D L N A N C Y B O Y O F A
S S N I F F E R A B O G G L E S
N I G T E H E R P E S L I M E T
O I L L Y O N A B O T T Y E T V
T H E M I G H T Y Q U I M O X R
T B U N N Y I T C H T I T T Y O
Y E S M A A M Y F A T S O C K S
P I M P L E P O P P E R T X Z A
D U V E T P O K E R T V S M O P
```

OPTICAL ILLUSION
Place your eyes about three inches from the photograph and open and close them very fast. A stuffed kangaroo will appear in front of the conductor.

"IT'S NOT ALL BEING NICE TO NIG NOGS"

A lot of people think that being a policeman these days is pansy stuff. Helping politicians across the street. Driving round in a Mini bloody Metro raising money for kidney machines. Community this, community that. And keep your truncheon at home to impress the girls.

But wandering round town in a blue uniform and a noddy hat is only a small part of a copper's work these days. In today's force the odds are you won't wear a uniform at all. Like the two constables in the **back** of the picture. Not so much as a tin badge in sight—you won't catch **them** teaching road safety down the Primary School.

They'll probably be at the rifle range. Or running a check through the computer. Or dressing up in kaftans and going to rock festivals.

Their own neighbours probably think they're discount carpet salesmen, or BBCTV reporters*.

If you're over seven feet tall and like wearing Harry Fenton suits, get in touch.

You'll find us across the road in the unmarked Granada, pretending to read the Daily Express.

*hard to tell them apart these days

POLICE

(Cont from Page 51)

personally responsible for the deaths of over 50,000 innocent civilians. He was captured by the British in the closing weeks of the war, and in common with many other senior SS officers given immunity from prosecution in return for a Rubens and two cases of Liebfraumilch. Equipped with a new name and identity, he entered Parliament in July 1945 at the age of 37. Although his poor command of English prevented him from speaking in public until almost ten years later, he rapidly found friends inside the Conservative Party, and achieved his first junior ministerial post under Eden in April 1955. He is married with four children, has a house in Kensington, a stud farm in Hampshire, and extensive estates in Scotland and Paraguay. Hobbies: house-painting, beer-tasting, leatherwork. Favourite composers: Wagner, Richard Strauss, Meatloaf. Majority at the last election: 17,643.

TONY BENN, LABOUR BRISTOL SOUTH-EAST, b 1925. 1925-77 irrelevant (mistakes, not denied, result of natural exuberance of youth, presence of Concorde work-force in Constituency etc). Born Again 1977; too modest to list achievements since that date. Favourite pastimes: being photographed drinking tea with workers (cf Thatcher, M., Jenkins, R.); wearing son's clothing on demo's; travelling on trains; thanking people for inviting him. Least favourite pastimes: sharing sleeper compartment with Eric Heffer; thinking of things to say to people you don't know in the back of taxis; removing the matted hair from the inside of the bath plug. Publications include: "The Way In: edited speeches to the Glasgow Campaign Against Editing Group, 1977-9"; "Getting Out: The effects of weather bias on the outcome of Trade Union meetings held in the open air, 1978-80" (ed C Bevin from two letters to Labour Weekly plus a new introduction dictated over the phone by the author); "The Next Step: The Monopoly Threat to Tea-Bags in the Nineties" (transcribed from a talk given by the author on Radio 4's "Today" programme). Address: The Big House, Holland Park Avenue; the Pied-a-Terre, Near Bristol Parkway, Avon.

SIR PETER BONEGARTE-FLATT-JONES, CONSERVATIVE, MALLAIG AND MORAR, b 1903, only son of **either** the late Brigadier General Sir Z de St Terence Bonegart-Shelffe **or** Lance Corporal Stanley Culvert, RASC and Lady Bryony Bonegarte-Jones-Flatt-Jones (nee Trezszhniszki), of The Old Kennel, LochNaGelty, Bath-on-Spey, Morayshire. Educ The Kennel School, Bath-on-Spey; Bishop Blunt's, Faversham; Harrow (Nippers' Colt 1919-20; Roger's Lay 1921-6; Longtrousers 1926-31; Senior School Probationer 1931-37; Runner-Up, IVth Form Nature Study Project, 1938; also 3rd XV Touch Judge 1931-37, 2nd XV Tour of Germany 1938; Mr Willoughby's Favourite, 1927-31, 1934). Education interrupted by outbreak of 2nd World War, volunteered for service as Honorary Padre, Nairobi Golf Club (decorated 1941, re-decorated 1951, 1959, 1972); retired hurt 1946, returned to Britain on the death of his father in 1951. Succeeded St Terence as Conservative and Onanist MP for Mallaig and Morar after by-election. Introduced Retention of

Restaurant Cars Beyond Fort William Bill (1963); leading member of the Well At Least A Buffet Car group of Scottish Tories. Address: Cubicle 9, The Superloo, Euston Station, London W1; or The Old Kennel, Bath-On-Spey.

THE RT HON JOAN BORROW PC, LABOUR FLATSANDEL & CHUDDLE, b 1935, eldest daughter of Professor Thomas Borrow and Dr Felicity Bapstein, The Blue House, Highgate London N1. Educ Highgate College for Girls (Head Girl 1950), Lady Margaret Hall, Oxford (MA), LSE (PhD, D Lit). Married, 1957, Dr Richard Book (m dissolved 1959). Elected Member for Flatsandel and Chuddle, 1964. Founder member, Commons Campaign For Soft Tissue In Ladies Toilets (1965); appointed Family Planning Minister (Oct 1965), resigned in protest over Peruvian Land Reform delays (1966); Chairperson, House of Commons Select Committee on Woman's Clothing in the Third World (1966), resigned in protest over sexism in Russian sport (Jan 1967); Minister Without Portfolio (Feb 1967), resigned in protest at colour of office carpet (June 1967); Minister for Underseas Aid and Negotiations (1969), resigned seven times in 4 months, still disputing redundancy terms when govt fell (1970). Set up Labour for Women in Labour (1971), subsequently started court proceedings against herself for alleged self-dismissal (1972). Resigned in anticipation of her selection as Minister for Community Awareness (1974); also as Legate Plenipotentiary to the 1975 UN Conference on Feminist Alternatives to Childbirth: meanwhile suspended for provoking unparliamentary language.* Publications (all in progress): 'Lesbians and the Struggle for Palestine'; 'The Politics of Sexuality in Local Government Housing Allocations 1967-9'; 'The Truth About Harold Wilson' (13 vols); 'Hair Care Without Combs'. Address: mind your own bloody business.

DR RHODES BOYSON, CONSERVATIVE BRENT NORTH, b 1925 of honest yeoman stock, we never had much but we went to Church on Sundays and didn't expect anyone else to help us out, especially not after Uncle Herbert died and left us his mantel clock and bicycle. I've still got them, both British, still in perfect working order, the housemaid oils them once a week. My father was a great believer in education, every Sunday we'd have to recite the bible by heart or he'd tie us to the sideboard and set to work with the horsewhip. A British horsewhip, that, beautiful workmanship, still as good as the day it was made. He taught me a lot, my father. He taught me to control my bowels. He taught me that it's a better bet to kick a man when he's down than it is to kick him when he's standing up. The only real tragedy of my life is that he died before he'd had time to teach me to shave. Now this Parliament is coming to an end, and a lot of you won't be coming back next session: a lot of you will be starting out in the real world, alone. I don't see what's so funny about that, Kinnock. Perhaps you'd like to come up here to the dispatch box and tell us what you find so funny about it. Who threw that? Come on, own up. Joseph, you look **pathetic**. Now come on. I don't mind waiting.

REGINALD CLIPP, LABOUR, MONKHOUSE, b 1938, son of Terry and Bessy Clipp, Foundry Gate Mansions, Smethwick. Educ (to age 9) Oldbury Church of England Primary School. Taken out of school when father left home and ran off with Sunday School teacher leaving mother to bring up 23 children alone, 1947. Worked nights at the steelworks, did milk and newspaper rounds, washed house, taught children to shoplift, emptied the earth closet (by hand), peeled potatoes, cooked gruel over humble fire of dried dog-turds, all we could afford, dug garden, gave hand-relief to landlord to protect ill mother, read too much Dickens ("Illustrated Classics" edition). National Service, Aden and Malaya, 1957-9. On return joined National Union of Newspaper Printers as full-time membership persuader and picket PE instructor. Secretary, Monkhouse Labour Party, 1960-63, with Union support. Elected MP 1964, with even more Union support. First MP to raise 1000 points of order in a single session (1967). Suspended (1969) for calling the Speaker a "fascist fart"; (1971) for calling Mr Heath "a typical fxxxing Oxbridge shirt-lifter"; (1972) for refusing to change his socks when requested to do so by an Official of the House; (1977) for exposing himself to the wife of the American Ambassador; (1981) for setting fire to an effigy of Mrs Thatcher in the Lobby; (1982) for eating a fish supper in the chamber (June), for damaging a stamp machine (August), for failure to clear up a committee room following celebrations to mark the 2nd Anniversary of the Nicaraguan Revolution (November); (1983) for referring to Princess Diana as "that aristocratic cock-teaser" (Feb), for urinating over the statue of Winston Churchill (April). Address: Flat 6B, Peaspudding Mansions, Pimlico; c/o Mrs O'Flaggharty, Viaduct Prospect, Monkhouse, Notts.

THE RT HON KENNETH JOHN CULVERT P.C., LABOUR, BRIGINSHAW, b 1921, fourth son of the late Stanley Culvert and Margaret Enid Jane Culvert (nee Tartsbottom), Haugh End Lane, Sowerby Bridge, West Yorks. Educ Haugh End Lane Primary School, Elland Grammar School (Cripps Scholar, 1932, Walter Horridge Essay Gold Medallist 1933, Secretary, Cub Section, Huddersfield and District Stamp Collecting Society, 1932-; Victor Ludorum, Elland Junior Travelling Chess League, 1934; Inventor of a new Patent Method of Repairing Spectacle Frames with Elastoplast, 1935; quarter-finalist, West Riding Osmiroid Owners Association Spelling Bee, 1937). WEA Exhibitioner, St Johns College, Oxford, 1935, active in Methodist Ramblers Group, Railway Modellers Tea Circle, Esperanto Association during first year, at end of which went for bicycling holiday in Lake District with Betty Murgatroyde, who subsequently married someone else (but ten years later became engaged to her sister Nora). Following term joined University Labour Party, Oxford Union, Friends of the Spanish Republic, 'Health and Efficiency' Book Club, year after elected Treasurer of Union, President of Labour Club, graduated with Triple First in PPE, got drunk with Denis Healey and Richard Crossman, arrested when prank with lavatory seat and dean's dog went wrong, fined 1/3d plus cost of fitting dog

On arrival at the polling station voters are welcomed by a colonel in dark glasses and presented with a free complimentary kebab before signing a statement confirming that they have not been subjected to any pressure or intimidation. Their limbs are then counted and a receipt issued. At this stage unsuccessful voters are eliminated and the remainder invited to sign a further disclaimer confirming the authenticity of their earlier statement, or to send back the kebab uneaten within seven days and have their children returned in full. While all this is going on the colonel goes on TV and declares himself President For Life.

LIECHTENSTEIN

Candidates inspect the ballot box containing the country's 4 popular votes before the count begins.

SUDAN

The task of collecting ballot-boxes from the outlying polling booths can take up to seventeen years. Here nominations for the 1976 municipal elections approach Khartoum in the spring of 1983.

FRANCE

French Polling Stations are very different to English ones. In France children are allowed inside, and a voter may dawdle for hours in his booth reading long pretentious novels over a citron pressé, making love to his mistress or simply pissing on the floor while reading the advertisements.

FIJI

The first voter who puts his ballot paper into the correct slot becomes Prime Minister.

ITALY

The most unusual election ever held took place in the small Italian village of Paldino in 1965 when, contrary to democratic tradition, voters were asked to mark their selections with a '✓' instead of an 'X'. To this day no one knows why . . . not even the candidates who were . . .

DURE	
TAMPA	
BOLLO	
PHU	
NIKKAELASTI	

Sgnr. Nikkaelasti objected to using the '✓' but was overruled.

ZAIRE

The franchise is open to anyone who owns a Mercedes or a Sanyo portable music centre, although candidates must be employees or relatives of the President. The country prides itself on its secret ballots. On arrival at the polling station voters are issued with two coloured balls, one representing the government, the other the opposition. Once inside the booth they place the ball of their choice in the ballot box, and on exiting return the unused ball to a member of the State Security Police.

COUNTRIES VOTE

Secretary of State Jim Prior checks prices with a vote-seller in Belfast City Market during the 1982 Assembly Elections.

NORTHERN IRELAND

HOLLAND

The Dutch have since 1957 used their own variation of the Multiple-entry Proportionate Transferable Preference Quota System, originally devised to help cross-index public library reminder cards in Denmark. Each of Holland's 493 political parties fields an identical number of candidates, who parade through the main square of the Hague in huge chicken costumes and attempt to balance on top of each other while standing in a child's paddling pool and trying not to listen to what Stuart Hall is saying. The voters are then required to remove their trousers and have their cheeks counted by a lecherous Italian in a loud blazer.

RUSSIA

An awful moment for President Brezhnev, as he struggles to recall which party he was going to vote for in the 1976 Russian General Election.

GUATEMALA

Guatemala. A returning officer with some of the "spoiled papers" he had to confiscate from the wallets of voters arriving at the polling station.

The conduct of elections is contracted out to the National Lottery, who are licensed to hawk ballot papers in multiples of ten in the streets of Guatemala City. Each ballot paper contains the name of an army general which is revealed by scraping the surface with a twenty centavos piece. The results of the coup are published in the press, and winning voters entitled to spend six months at a CIA training camp in Georgia.

NEW ZEALAND

The State Opening of Parliament.

NEPAL

Nepal is a theocracy, ruled over by the Divine Lanka. When the incumbent dies, a team of 73 monks is despatched to Tibet to discover his successor, following a complicated procedure of omens and signs. The new Lanka, once discovered, is ceremonially drugged, blinded and lobotomised before being placed on a cushion in the royal palace in Khatmandu and persuaded to smile silently at visitors while the monks get on with running the country.

58

Dr. David's Column

TEBBITISM–IS THERE A CURE?

During the exciting fervour of the run-up to the general election in 1979 a team of highly qualified parapsychoanalysts, parapsychotherapists, para-psychopathologists and paratroopers were commissioned by the TUC to investigate the possibilities of a successful cure for Tebbitism. Their brief was quite simple—capture a compulsive Tebbitic and, using all reasonable means at their disposal and without using actual violence well not a lot of violence, cure him. The results of the experiment, up till now a closely guarded secret, are given in detail below. But first, what is Tebbitism?

Tebbitism, in its mildest form, is the compulsive urge to vote for the Rt. Hon. Norman Tebbit at elections, and in its most chronic form compels the sufferer to stick a 'Vote Norman Tebbit' leaflet in the front bedroom window. The disease, affecting people living mainly in Chingford (although cases have been discovered living as far away as just outside Chingford) has been analysed as a psychotic illness rather than, as was once thought, invisible leprosy.

THE EXPERIMENT. Mr X, a fiction writer on the 'Daily Express', had all the symptoms of Tebbitism ie; beating his mother, asking the window cleaner for a receipt, wearing bicycle clips at funerals etc. He volunteered for the experiment on a money back if not entirely satisfied basis. The experiment began three weeks before election day and was based on the Sir Keith Foaming theory that is: When a person is wrapped in a warm straight-jacket, legs tied together with 5-amp flex, isolated inside a 'Slumberdream' padded cell and kept entirely ignorant of any Conservative election news or propaganda until after the election then that person must be me. This they did and the following is an exact copy of the report on the patient's reactions to treatment after being carefully observed over a period of twenty-one days.

THE REPORT

DAY 1 Patient persistently screaming for his solicitor.

DAY 2 Patient's lips sealed with tape.

DAY 3 Patient persistently screaming for his mmmmmmmmmm.

DAY 4 Day off.

DAY 5 FIRST SIGNS OF A BREAKTHROUGH. Patient shares his rusk with a crippled canary.

DAY 6 Patient showing remarkable improvement—new hair is sprouting in the bald patches (Tebbipaecia) and his eyeballs have stopped spinning.

DAY 7 Using straw from his mattress patient has built a canary cage with his toes.

DAY 8 Canary persistently whistling for it's solicitor. Patient makes further progress—asks for a Daily Mirror.

DAY 9 Another crippled canary arrives.

Contd. on page 67

WHO OWNS BRITAIN?

Twenty years ago, 84% of the wealth of Britain was owned by just 7% of the population. 48.3% of dogs were owned by only 61.7% of women. Fewer than 7% of the adult population had *ever* succeeded in scraping off that goo that's left on the side of the Nescafé jar once you've washed off the label. .000000001% of university graduates knew their own post-codes.

Today all that has changed. 85% of the wealth is owned by 6.93% of the population, under a variety of holding companies (see map), and the number of people who know their post-codes has almost doubled. Other statistics to emerge from the 1981 census:

*Vicars are 32 times as likely to own Saabs as the rest of the population.

*The number of people who make homosexual jokes about the Liberal Party has fallen 11% in five years.

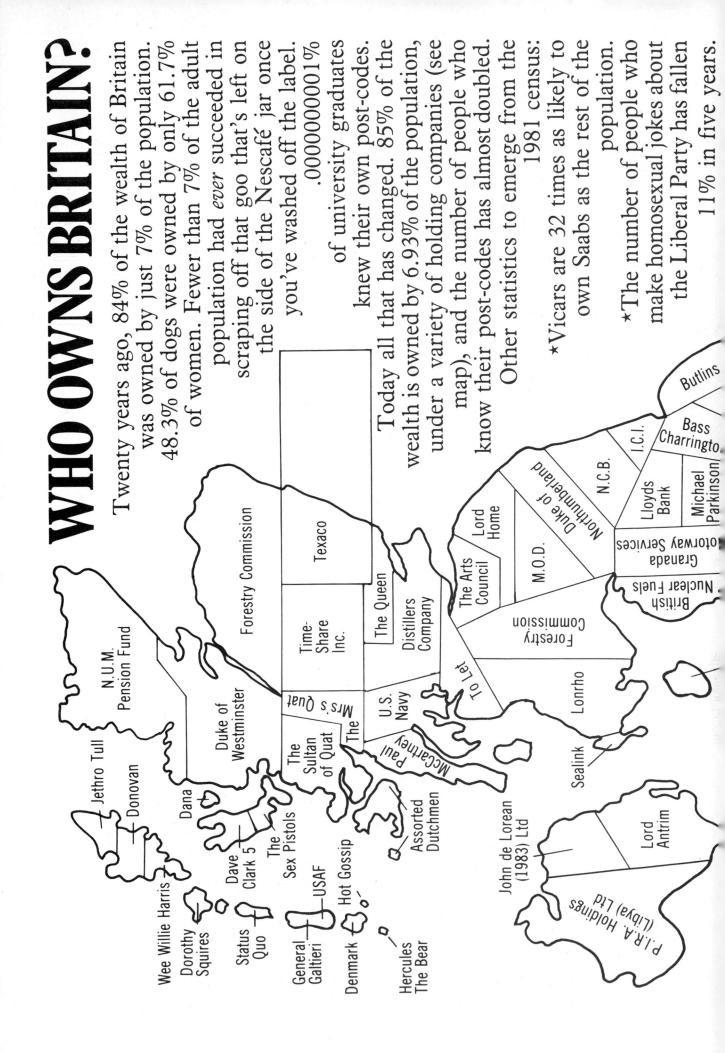

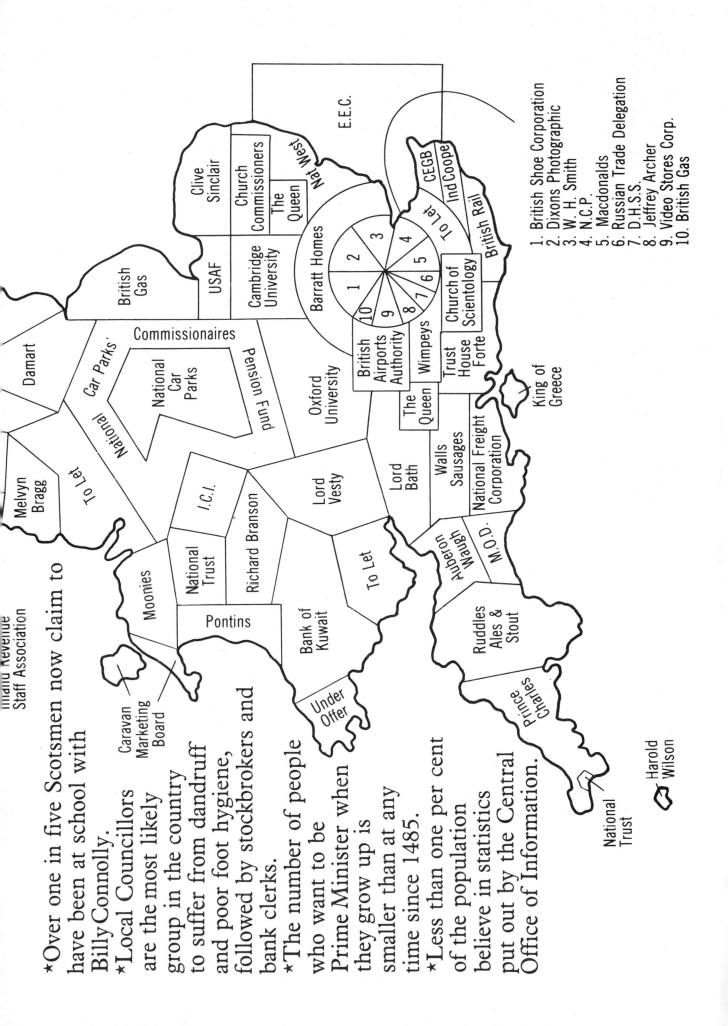

*Over one in five Scotsmen now claim to have been at school with Billy Connolly.

*Local Councillors are the most likely group in the country to suffer from dandruff and poor foot hygiene, followed by stockbrokers and bank clerks.

*The number of people who want to be Prime Minister when they grow up is smaller than at any time since 1485.

*Less than one per cent of the population believe in statistics put out by the Central Office of Information.

1. British Shoe Corporation
2. Dixons Photographic
3. W. H. Smith
4. N.C.P.
5. Macdonalds
6. Russian Trade Delegation
7. D.H.S.S.
8. Jeffrey Archer
9. Video Stores Corp.
10. British Gas

PARLIAMENTARY PERKS

Upon election every MP, regardless of age, sex or colour automatically gets:
* Unlimited air, rail and coach travel within the UK
* A Disabled Driver *or* CD sticker to put in the back of his car
* Two white nylon *or* one Viyella check shirt plus non-matching tie
* One knee-length sheepskin car-coat *or* a lightweight polyester raincoat and tartan scarf; and a pair of brown brogues
* Office equipment, to include: two pub ashtrays; one second-hand stapler; an unillustrated Agricultural Supplier's wall calendar; a small bakelite desk-tidy containing a ½p stamp, two drawing pins, and a quantity of what looks like navel fluff; a card bearing the phone number of a mini-cab firm that went out of business in 1967; an elderly cheese sandwich still in its original Clingwrap; a buff envelope containing the operating instructions for a vacuum cleaner; and one empty Lambs Navy Rum miniature.
* Enough expensive House of Commons notepaper to keep a family of nine in drawing materials for five years
* A small radio transmitter, code-book and miniature camera
* A forged photograph of him- or herself on a sofa with *either* Clem Attlee *or* Winston Churchill; or of a small child of the appropriate sex standing outside 10 Downing Street
* A Voucher entitling the bearer to write an article on the eccentricities of foreign hotel staff for *either* 'Punch' *or* 'High Life' while Sheridan Morley is on holiday
* Enough daily newspapers to cover a shelf to a depth of seven inches
* A Secretary in her early thirties who is divorced and looking for somewhere to live

PRIVILEGES

Statute law grants MPs a number of legal immunities, including:
* Freedom from most forms of prosecution, particularly if they often meet the Chief Constable socially. These rights may however be suspended immediately before a parliamentary debate on police pay and conditions.
* The right, without any other explanation, to refuse an invitation to appear on 'Stop The Week' or 'Call My Bluff' ; and to decline to taste anything offered to them in the street by Esther Rantzen.
* The right not to close the communicating door after them on trains when making their way to the buffet car or toilet.
* The option not to tell Customs Officers where they are going on holiday or how old their children are.
* MPs are not obliged to take part in aerobics on Waterloo Station when requested to do so.
* Since 1653 Members of both Houses have been absolved from the obligation to smile at clergymen in public places.
* MPs are free to continue holding 'consultations' on licensed premises with whomsoever they please outwith the normal licensing hours, and additionally to purchase alcoholic substances for visiting police officers on such premises when it may seem appropriate; but they are requested to refrain from spitting or singing in the saloon unless accompanied by an ill-tempered alsatian.

HOW AN MP's INCOME BREAKS DOWN

INCOME

Salary	13,950
Allowances:	
Nods and Winks	5,623
Appearance fees	2,320
Sale of postcards and souvenirs	1
Fees for Use of Name on Company Prospectuses etc	7,437
Sub-letting of Westminster office	4,164
Return of empties	1,266
"Secretarial"	8,480
Serialisation of Memoirs	45
Sale of Offices etc	11,455
Opening fetes, supermarkets etc	850
Accommodation	4,903
Travel	3,500
Protective clothing	756
Disappearance fees	1,890
Luck Money	155
Total income:	**£66,795**

EXPENDITURE

Rent to mother	450
Payments to lookalikes	960
Accommodation address	50
Purchase of constituency street-map	0.45
Purchase of constituency in first place	15,000
Letter to constituent	0.42
Payments to journalists Reciprocal hospitality to PR's for lunches received	2,800
	1
Own lunches (est.)	2
Divorce costs	750
Hush money	7,653
Gratuities to Man on Door who gets taxis	5
Engagement rings (×17)	21
Bus fares	105
Total Expenditure	**32,301.87**
	66,795
Depreciation of Credibility (written off)	34,493.12
Balance	**£0.01**

THE HOUSE & CHAMBER
POT POURRI

UNPARLIAMENTARY LANGUAGE

Brownhatter	Hockney
Jewboy	Bollard-brain
Spas	Noggin
Nancy	Whimp
Whoremonger	Pongy-pants
Snotsucker	Quim
Four-eyes	Lettuce-leaf
Soggy-toast	Scots baboon
Pillock-biter	You-and-whose-army
Tebbit	Milksop
Rubberlips	Wang-tickler
Nozzer	Putty-lugs
Pathetic little verruca	Dogshagger
Pigeonballs	Carrot-top
Englander Schweinhunt	Great Nob
Taffy	Slugnipples
Jobsworth	Houmous-pants
Queue-jumper	Prick-parer
Tart	Weasel
Hinny	Brothersucker
Frump	Mother
Pussy-licker	Seat-sniffer
Schmuckface	Pudding-botty
Pilchard-face	Sailor
Faggot-snatcher	

PRINCIPAL OFFICERS OF THE PALACE OF WESTMINSTER

Mr Speaker's Mate	Rear Admiral Sir Terence Sledge DBE
Mrs Speaker's Mate	The Rt Hon Peter Hint Bt
Black Rod	The Duke of Earl
White Rod	V.D.U. de St J. Hum PQR.STU, VC
Green Rod	Hewison Mi
Yeoman Ushers of the Rods	John Julius Norwich Christopher Caius Esher Victor Matthews Esq and members of the BBC Chorus
Keeper of the Ayes and Nays	Sir Hamish Quink of That Ink
Caterer At Arms	B. Brush
Keeper of the Hats of Bute	Mrs Adams, 17, The Brae, Tighnabruich
Keeper of the Coughs	Imam Mustaffa Mahmet El Llwellyn-Jones DC
Retainer of Hansoms in Perpetuity	Sgt Willis
Recorder of Means and Ends	Lt Colonel Tubby Trodd
Principal Stranger	Wayne Sleep
Spear carrier	Lord George Brown
Vicar	Russ Abbott
Policeman	Oliver Reed

With
The Yvonne Littlewood Dancers
Ken Ellis and Toby
The Amazing Marvel
The Bavarian State Finger-puppets
Rod Hull and Oxo
Bobby Crush

BACKGROUND ON MPs
PREVIOUS PROFESSIONS

	CON	LAB	ALLIANCE	OTHER
Something in the City	209	1	3	—
Something at a Polytechnic	1	137	2	—
Queen's Counsel	23	23	1	—
Council Queens	1	7	3	—
Anglia TV Quizmasters	17	—	—	—
Schoolfriends of Ludovic Kennedy	187	161	21	4
Swineherds	—	—	2	1
Transatlantic yachtsmen	—	—	—	3
Neither of the above	7	3	1	6
"Journalists"	3	45	6	—
Gourmets	15	—	15	—
Marxist homosexuals	8	—	—	—
Double-glazing consultants	—	—	3	—
Brewer's reps	17	—	—	—
Football referees	—	11	—	1

COMMONEST MIDDLE NAMES

	CON	LAB	ALLIANCE	OTHER
1	Hardress	Arthur	John	Llanydafffl
2	Borage	Bertram	William	Rioradhic IV
3	Pending	Bevan	Richard	Madge
4	de Zouche-Quiggly	Ebeneezer	Henry	Ilk
5	Mufffin	Nancy	Peter	In-tray
6	Ammoroso	Whippet	—	The Post
7	Axminster	Bevin	—	—
8	Sanyo Hi-Fi	Trot	—	—
9	Fifi	Illyushin	—	—
10	Battenberg	Borage	—	—

WHY ARE THERE SO FEW WOMEN MPs

Out of 635 MPs, an astonishing 614 are men, and only eleven are women.* Why is this? One school of thought believes it is due to the deeply ingrained conservatism of all party selection procedures, the sexist attitudes of local committees and a reluctance amongst the electorate to believe that women are capable of taking decisions.

The true facts are that women do not become MPs (1) because very few of them are power-mad arrogant maniacs with homosexual tendencies, lisps, an inability to listen and dreadful taste in suits and (2) because they can't see what is such a big deal about spending the waking hours kissing babies and walking around shopping precincts.

*The remainder are made up as follows: Dame Judith Hart, Edward Heath (who is not made up at all), one insect (Peter Shore), Cyril Smith (who is a Sofa from the planet Zillon), and five others whose sex cannot be determined until they actually turn up at Westminster.

NB. Mrs Thatcher counts as ten men **or** an alligator.

THERE'S NOTHING DAVE CAN'T FIX

Tighten the odd screw, replace a few old nuts, a drop of oil in the right place, and the machine's back on the road again, much the way it was in Grandad Grimond's day.

But when it comes to looking after his own future, Dave's got bigger plans. That's why he's joined

THE ALLIANCE

if we haven't got a policy to suit you, we'll run one up for you on the spot.

LAUGH WITH CONFIDENCE

"For years I never opened my mouth in public, afraid of what might come out. And I don't just mean my opinions!
Then a friend suggested I try new Heseltine's GUMGUM—and now Denture Adventures are a thing of the past."
new Heseltine's

RETURNING OFFICERS
– 12 things you never wanted to know

1 HOW MANY RETURNING OFFICERS ARE THERE?
609.

2 WHEN WERE THEY BORN?
November 7th 1928.

3 WHERE WERE THEY EDUCATED?
King Athelgarde's Grammar School, Crawley.

4 WHAT DID THEY DO IN THE WAR?
Because Returning Officers look older than they are, many claim to have seen action with the Royal Army Service Corps in North Yorkshire. In fact they were still at school.

5 DO THEY WEAR GLASSES?
Yes, although they remove them shortly before the election result is declared to signal to television producers that something is about to happen. The Returning Officer will not put his glasses on again until satisfied in his own mind that he is live on screen. The Putting On Of The Glasses is an important moment in the reading of the result, and can last up to seven minutes.

6 WHAT ARE THEIR HOBBIES?
Caravanning, Greenhouses, Daily Telegraph Crosswords.

7 WHAT DO THEY DRINK IN PUBS?
Half pints of beer.

8 WHAT DO THEY DRINK AT HOME?
Mateus Rosé.

9 WHAT ARE THEIR FAVOURITE PERIODICALS?
"Punch", "What Caravan", "Teen Clit".

10 WHAT DO THEY ENJOY MOST ON TV?
"The Two Ronnies", especially the bits set at cocktail parties; "Mastermind"; and documentaries in which lions, jackals etc dismember innocent deer, ducks etc.

11 HOW ARE THEIR CHILDREN CONCEIVED?
Returning Officers are notoriously under-sexed; and Returning Officers' wives are only fertile for a maximum of eleven minutes a year. Although precise details of the mating rituals are covered by the Official Secrets Act, successful "bonding" is understood to be a complex and time-consuming process (see below).

12 WHAT DO RETURNING OFFICERS DO BETWEEN ELECTIONS?
See above (11).

REPRESENTATION OF THE PEOPLE ACT (1982) APPENDIX CCXXXIVL: DUTIES OF THE RETURNING OFFICER UPON DECLARING THE RESULT OF A PARLIAMENTARY ELECTION

At such time as the counting of votes shall apparently be complete, the Returning Officer or his deputy shall arrange for a further supply of uncounted papers to be produced and counted; and shall instruct his clerks to arrange for the *already* counted papers to be displayed in a way designed to confuse the waiting candidates and any journalists or bookmakers present as to the likely outcome of the poll; and shall wink encouragingly at any unsuccessful candidate who may catch his eye. Which task completed he shall make his way to the platform together with the candidates, and a little man in a tweed jacket shall lean in front of him and strike the microphones, uttering the words "testes, testes, one two three", at which the Returning Officer shall cough thrice.

Then shall the Returning Officer put on his spectacles and extract from his pocket a small piece of paper on which is written EITHER his wife's shopping list OR the dimensions of the area of bathroom floor which he proposes to re-tile. Which piece of paper he shall then dispose of in a way he is unlikely to be able subsequently to recall, to his own OR his wife's considerable irritation: and shall extract a second piece of paper on which has been inscribed the result of the election.

J.D. Robinson (Islington) Britain's first entirely Gay returning officer.

Thanks to the Youth Opportunities Programme, Wolverhampton South West now has over 3,500 trainee returning officers.

IS MAGGIE THATCHER A RUSSIAN SPY?

Before you cast your vote at this crucial election we ask you to stop—and consider this burning question . . .

IS MRS THATCHER A RUSSIAN SPY?

Below we put before you a number of seemingly innocent facts concerning our prime minister.
Are they a damning indictment of Mrs Thatcher's true politics or are they just innocent coincidences? You are the judge.

THE VERDICT IS YOURS

● Her very first words were "Da-Da". (Da-Da is Russian for yes-yes)
● She wears RED lipstick.
● When God opened his beauty salon she was last in. (Last in is an anagram of Stalin)
● She helped in her father's grocery shop. The shop sold onions. (The Kremlin towers are shaped like onions)
● She does all her own spring cleaning including ironing the curtains. (Russia is behind the iron curtain)

● She's got varicose veins on her legs. (Or are they aerials running from a secretly hidden transmitter?)
● She made Michael Heseltine minister for defence. (She must be on their side)

Contd. from page 59

DAY 10 A cure seems imminent—patient is humming The Red Flag as he works on another canary cage.
DAY 11 Patient now feeding and training 21 crippled canaries and almost completed 9th cage.
DAY 12 Patient asks for pin-ups of Vanessa Redgrave and Dame Judith Hart. Starts building cage for crippled New Hebridean Puffin.

DAY 13 Patient now corresponding with Tony Benn and Sir Peter Scott. 317 crippled canaries, a mince of crippled New Hebridean Puffins and a pair of crippled Birds of Paradise all whistling The Red Flag.
DAY 14 Patient asks for a supply of dead mice for the crippled Owls.
DAY 15 Decision day—should we register the world's first padded aviary with the patents office.

Contd. on page 73

The History of Democracy

The political system on which our own democracy is based really began in Ancient Greece, a country where three-quarters of the population were slaves and babies were left out on the hillside to die.

All citizens were entitled to vote provided that they:
—were over twenty-one
—owned a hypoteneuse
—lent Socrates their bum-boy every now and then.

On election day all twenty-five citizens would stroll down to the market-place (or 'kleftiko') where two large vases (or 'kebabi') were placed side by side on the pavement ('pave-mento'). Each citizen would then cast a little ball of dung (or 'psephos')* into the vase of his choice (or 'avgolemoni'). These were then counted up, where-upon the (or 'e') citizens got into their chariots, drove over to the Oracle at Delphi and asked it what to do. At this point an old bat would come out of the cave with twigs in her hair and dribble all down her dress and give her answer, usually along the lines of 'The long geese are flying low this month' or some other useful hint, after which it would be pretty obvious who had won.

The returning officer was then despatched from Marathon to run to Athens (a distance of 27½ miles) announce the result and die—for this reason the returning officer was traditionally a boring little man with a droning voice, a heart condition, and a silly middle name who would otherwise be of no use whatsoever to the community. Making such people returning officers saved cluttering up the hillsides—leaving plenty of room for babies, old folk and heterosexuals.

*the origin of the word 'psephologist'

The First 'MP'

The first real 'MP' was Alexander the Great. After becoming the youngest 'President of the Oxford Union' in history, he entered local politics at the age of twelve and, in a brilliant campaign covering 156 cities, he swept to power — completely slaughtering his rivals in a 25,000-sided contest. By the age of 32 he was 'MP' for the largest 'constitu-ency' in the world — repre-senting Mesopotamia, Macedon, Thrace, Epirus, Phrygia, Armenia, most of Egypt and the Hindu Kush: an area which, under the recommenda-tions of the 'Boundary Commission' in 327 BC, became known as the Macedonian Empire, and which Alexander the Great represented until his death forty-five minutes later.

How did he do it? By a remarkable combination of charm, good looks, intel-ligence, hard work, lying through his teeth and kill-ing people.

Democracy in Britain

Since 1215 when King John was cast adrift on an island in the Thames with-out any jewels until he agreed to sign the Magna Carta, Britain has been known as the Mother of Parliaments. This means that we are better than everyone else, and our system of government has allowed us to go on to invent penicillin, the hover-craft and Martin Webster. Our system of democracy is completely unique and has been followed all over the world. The American Way of Democracy, which is based on the idea that the party which has the most balloons wins, has, by contrast, produced nothing of value except chewing gum, herpes and certain parts of Marilyn Monroe. The French, who have been governed by a suc-cession of stunted little dictators with piles, elderly nancy boys in curly wigs and men with big noses and Tommy Cooper hats, still think it's smart to piss in the street. And the less said about the Germans the better.

But British democracy hasn't all been plain sail-ing. In the eighteenth and nineteenth centuries Par-liament was filled with MP's from the so-called 'rotten boroughs'. Such men were often incredibly old and boring. Sometimes they didn't speak in the Commons for years. Many owned suspiciously large houses in the country. Others would leave their clothes on the beach and disappear to Australia without so much as a by-your-leave. But the Great Reform Bill of 1832 sorted all this kind of thing out and made it legal.

In Britain today everyone over the age of eighteen is allowed to vote if they can be bothered—except for the Royal Family, Peers of the Realm, lunatics and Desmond Wilcox. Esther Rantzen *is* allowed to vote providing she does it quietly and tries not to leave her after-birth all over the polling-booth.

The General Election of 1665

Daniel Defoe's classic book "Journal of the Election Year" tells us much about how elections were conducted in the 17th Century. Defoe relates how he set off for his nearest polling station at Tewkesbury — three days' ride away — to vote in the General Election of 19th June 1665. He took with him his wife, children and servants as well as several head of cattle. These last were a regrettable mistake, for, mishearing the voting instructions from the town-crier, he was labouring under the impression that in order to register his vote he was obliged to place an ox next to the candidate of his choice.

Having voted, Defoe returned home. He was determined not to go to bed before hearing the result of the election, and was rewarded by the traditionally swift constituency of Bath declaring first* on the 10th August. Thereafter the pace became a little less hectic, but Defoe doggedly stayed up until the turn of the year, retiring to bed on the 4th January 1666 — the final result still undecided — a broken man.

*Whig hold

Louis XVIIVXXII of France.

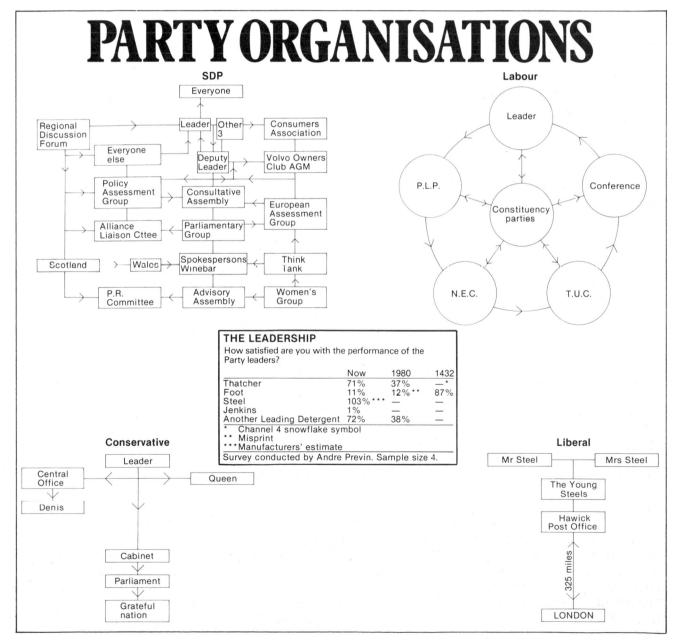

PARTY ORGANISATIONS

SDP

Everyone

Regional Discussion Forum → Leader → Other 3 → Consumers Association

Everyone else → Deputy Leader → Volvo Owners Club AGM

Policy Assessment Group → Consultative Assembly → European Assessment Group

Alliance Liaison Cttee → Parliamentary Group

Scotland → Wales → Spokespersons Winebar ← Think Tank

P.R. Committee ← Advisory Assembly ← Women's Group

Labour

Leader

P.L.P.

Conference

Constituency parties

N.E.C.

T.U.C.

THE LEADERSHIP

How satisfied are you with the performance of the Party leaders?

	Now	1980	1432
Thatcher	71%	37%	—*
Foot	11%	12%**	87%
Steel	103%***	—	—
Jenkins	1%	—	—
Another Leading Detergent	72%	38%	—

* Channel 4 snowflake symbol
** Misprint
***Manufacturers' estimate

Survey conducted by Andre Previn. Sample size 4.

Conservative

Leader

Central Office ← → Queen

Denis

Cabinet

Parliament

Grateful nation

Liberal

Mr Steel — Mrs Steel

The Young Steels

Hawick Post Office

325 miles

LONDON

TRA

It's hard to imagine in 1983 that there was a time—within recent memory—when politicians were expected to pay for their holidays out of their own pockets. When a backbencher was satisfied with two weeks in Tenby or a cruise on the Norfolk Broads.

But of course all that was before the Travel Revolution, before the jumbo jet, the package tour, the personalised leather-look passport holder with matching key fob and luggage tag, the hand combination travel-iron and rechargeable bedside light, the Evening Mail Readers Offer See The Magic Of Belgium's Bulb Fields In November By Barge And Bus For Only £346 Excluding Tax Insurance Travel And Accommodation Based On Eleven Sharing See Absolutely Minute Print At Bottom For Pitfalls*. And, of course, before the world's unspoilt places became cluttered up with plagues of free-loading Parliamentary Delegations, Euro-missions, Fact-finders, Fraternal Exchangers, Town-twinners, Election Observers and International Conference attenders who sit around in the bars of Holidays Inns wearing plastic name-clips and stealing the towels out of the bathrooms**.

But no single innovation over the past twenty years has done quite so much to transform the pattern of political holidays as the growth in what the trade calls Totalitarian Travel: the practice by which "strong" foreign governments hand out luxury holidays to any politician or journalist for a price which can be as little as a simple endorsement of the regime. There are an enormous number of these packages on the market now, catering for almost every taste.

So be sure to shop around. Will they pay for your wife or "secretary"? Are embarrassing

AVEL

photographs likely to crop up in the British Press? Is any actual work involved? Who else is likely to be on the trip? How far is the hotel from the beach? How much does it cost to send a postcard? Do most masseuses speak English? Will you have room for a sweet if you have two starters? Do they wrap a piece of paper round the toilet seat each time they clean the room? Can you stop over in Bangkok on the way back? And so on. You're also advised to take out Coup Insurance or Diplomatic Immunity.

For further details write to:

The Anglo-Libyan Stamp Collectors Guild, Kensington Palace Gardens, London W2.

His Excellency The Under-Pastry Cook, 'Papa Doc's' Haitian WholeFood Bar And Tractor Parts Export Agency, Perrymeade St, London SW8.

Mein Host, The Fantastically Free and Autonomous People's Homeland of Mtsetublgse-land, c/o South Africa House, The Strand, London WC1.

The Occupant, Blockhouse 489b, Street of The Glorious Concrete Pavement, Seoul, South Korea.

Kabul and District Rotary Club, PO Box 195, Kabul, Afghanistan.

The Welsh Development Agency, Government House, Cardiff, Daffffyd, Cymru.

Chad and District Amateur Operatic Society, 3, The Street, Chad EC7Q.

Friends of the Bulgar Umbrella, 186, Queen's Gate, London SW7.

*Isn't it odd how most people on coach tours wear glasses.
**You can't miss them: they're the only people in the world who still pay full price on aeroplanes and buy shirts in airport Duty Free shops.

PROPERTY FOR THE NEW MEMBER
STICKLAND & BRILLET
Partners

CASTLE MELMOTH. Edinburgh 314 miles. Reykjavik 6¼ miles. Kilnairnietoun 2¾ miles (take West Door out of Chinese Dining Room, village is eighth exit on left inside Conservatory behind Burmese Elm plantation).

BLOODY ENORMOUS PIECE OF EDWARDIAN INSANITY WITH VIEWS OF SUTHERLAND, PERTHSHIRE AND CROMARTY EASILY OBTAINED BY PEERING UNDER THE LINO.

124 Reception Rooms. 98 Dining Rooms. 70 Breakfast Rooms. 62 Brunch Rooms. 34 Luncheon Lobbies. Banqueting Hall. 19th Century Elevenses Chamber. Horlicks Gallery. 254 Bedrooms (28 still undiscovered) including 40 Horse-Boudoirs, 22 Double-Labrador Suites, 9 finely-appointed Hawk-Lofts with ensuite Rabbit-Hutches.

1 Bathroom. 3,507 Downstairs Loos are fully-stocked with Green Gumboots and Tweed Capes. Billiard Room. Snooker Room. Pool Room. Crazy Golf Hall. Indoor Rugby Pitch. Tennis Court. 100ft Ballroom. 200ft Racquet Room. Cue Store. Bat Belfry. Indoor Swimming Pool (Olympic Marathon Size) with own U-Boat Pen, and quaint Portuguese Fishing Community of charm and character. 16 Gun-Rooms. 2 Stag-Flensing Chambers. 8 Smoking Rooms. 12 Grill-Rooms. 3 Magnificent Torture-Chambers. 91 Kitchens (inc. 4 fish-farms, 6 abattoirs, 2 morgues, sandwich-maker).

44 Sculleries. 770 Cupboards Under The Stairs, each with Gas Meter, Broken Kite, Plastic Bin Liner Full of Clogs, Groundsheets and Old Biscuit Tins.

2 40ft x 30ft Officers Messes. 640 3in x ½in Dogs Messes. 36 Inner Sanctums. American Style Den. Trophy Room. Sellotape Closet. Lumber Room. Muesli

Store. 13,052 Inglenooks. Tea-Room. 12 Sitting Rooms. 8 Standing Rooms. 6 Kneeling Parlours. Crouching Closet. 3 Bending Over Backwards Cubby Holes. 12th Century Italian Piazza Parlour, with own fountain, cathedral. 180 Attics. 86 Junk Rooms. 64 Dust-Sheet Vestibules. Library. Public Baths. 6 Launderettes. 2 Job Centres. Haunted Grotto. Garotted Haunto. Persian Room. Japanese Restaurant (closed Suns). Heliport. 16 Vomitoriums. Another Bathroom. Bloody hell, and there's half a dozen more Gun-Rooms in here too. 8 Pheasantries. Unisex Hairdressers. Railway Turntable. Extensive Wine Cellars to be sold with 80 Elderly French Peasants with original feet. 124 Studies. Dairy. Garage for 36 Cars. In addition 1,574 further rooms That No-One Could Possibly Want. Outside Toilet.

Large Servants Quarters In Own Wing. Butlers Pantry. Cooks Solarium. Battery Skivvy Farm. 38 Maid-Closets. 40ft x 40ft Gardener-Pit. 6 Swineherd Huts. 9 Flunkey-Bins. 12 Groom-Punnets. Extensive Slave-Bunker. Cave for Chauffeur. Ghillie-Box. 52 Scullion-Cages. 5 Priest-Holes.

Stable Block. Home Farm of 13,000 Acres with own Trout Cannery, Pate Farm, Salmon-Meadows and Gooserie, situated roof of North Wing approx 3½ miles aft of main funnels. Salt Flats. Grouse Moor. 32 Werewolf Kennels. 56 Cottages, three small hotels, 9 pubs, Post Office, 3 Banks, 12 Bars, Second Class Lounge, Quoit Deck, Snowstorm Paperweight & Postcard Shop. FOR SALE BY PUBLIC AUCTION, PRIVATE TREATY OR BLOODY MIRACLE.

PUTTNAM HALL, WORCESTERSHIRE

Worcester-on-Sauce 4 miles. Lea 3½ miles. Perrins 2½ miles. Puttnam 35 yards.

DESIRABLE RURAL RESIDENCE SET ON 0.0003 ACRES (Summer Months).

A Superb Thatched Antheap in original condition, within fawning distance of magnificent Puttnam Hall, country seat of Lord Puttnam of Chariot. For the once-in-a-lifetime chance of being near to the great man, this breeze, compact dwelling is OFFERED FOR SALE FREEHOLD AT £8,775 o.n.o.

Applicants, who should be young, gifted and black, should apply IN WRITING, DURING THE HOURS OF DARKNESS ONLY to SOUWESTER, COGWIT & SPRUCE Partners of Epping. The successful applicant will be expected to put up with a man who looks suspiciously like Johnny Morris poking his willy through the roof on a regular basis.

PORTICO, WAINSCOT, TRELLIS Partners

A VERY FINE, WELL-APPOINTED FAMILY RESIDENCE SET IN 2½ ACRES OF LAND.

Study, south facing TREE, situated in heart of Sir Oswald Mosley Memorial Car Park, Fulham.

Ripe for imaginative conversion, this delightful old home is wood-panelled throughout. Would suit person who is fond of trees. 3/4 Bedrooms, 2 Bathrooms, Cloakroom, k&b would be nice but what can you expect for only £37,499.

OFFERS ARE INVITED FOR THIS INCREDIBLY DECENT ATTEMPT BY US TO CONTRIBUTE TO THE GENERAL WELL-BEING OF THE COMMUNITY

SLITHY, TOVES Ltd.

2 BEDROOM GARDEN FLAT, SOUTH KENSINGTON.

Tiny, unpleasant-smelling cellar with view of upstairs concrete coal bunker. Situated close to shops, near schools, underneath public transport etc, in South Kensington Avenue, Norwood SE55. Master Bedroom (8ft x 2ft), Smaller Bedroom (Behind sink-panel in Kitchen), Kitchen (in Wardrobe in Master Bedroom). Reception 50ft x 4ft with 19th Century Commissionaire at one end, conveniently placed outside front door. H&C running water in all rooms. Bathroom (planning permission available). Window (18in x ½in) £88,795.

GLOSSARY OF PARLIAMENTARY LANGUAGE

ABSE (n) The technical device whereby an MP is deemed to be in the Chamber when he is in fact elsewhere (physically or otherwise), so called because of the wooden abse, or boss, with which MPs traditionally remove their shoes without untying the laces during long debates.

BIFFEN (n) A wafer served with coffee in the lobby of the House; a lightweight, a thing of no worth: also, cllql, a buttock.

BOYSON (v) To verbally obstruct the passage of one smaller than oneself, to override the interest of a minority, normally in a queue.

CONCANNON (v) To speak without listening; to continue to speak after the rest of the Chamber has left; to speak to the wrong person in error.

DALYELL (adj) Beyond the ability of the audience to comprehend; passing all understanding.

FAULDS (n) A skin disease effecting the groin and lower torso, common among members from Midlands constituencies.

FOULKES (n) The small silver-embossed message pads on which members order their interval drinks before a debate.

GORST (n) A political assertion or statement so extreme that it is received in total silence and disbelief; hence, the momentary vacuum which precedes uproar in the House.

GOW (n) A low chant in unison, in which the word is repeated over and over by Members to indicate their opinion that a speaker is expressing views which are not his own, but handed down to him by his betters; a plant; a gopher; a pan-scrubber; a beer-mat; a dustbin-liner; a device for shaving dogs' legs; an uneaten hamburger bun; a chair which is left empty because broken.

HAVERS (n) The arrangement of wooden slats in the room above the Sanitorium in which MPs keep their Tuck Boxes.

HAYHOE (n) The ritual ducking in a bath of port which new Members are required to undergo before gaining access to Havers (see above).

JESSEL (n) One who changes parties without telling anyone (or being noticed).

LAMONT (v) To decry publicly a policy or action which one is privately in favour of.

LESTOR (n) A down-to-earth overcoat or rainproof put on by politicians when campaigning in the open air.

MABON (adj) Lacking in humour; also (v), to laugh at a joke one has clearly not understood.

McCUSKER (v) Lit: to hide behind thick spectacles; hence, to be all things to all men (cf KINNOCK).

MULLEY (adj) Lukewarm; bulbous (of fish); having the consistency of creme caramel; fungoid; flat, appearing to have no visible horizon; tending to adhere to the soles of shoes; having the texture of a picked pig's foot; Belgian-looking (hence cllql Brummie); pear-bottomed; pink-nippled; glandulous when humid; false-toothed; inadvertently flatulent; odd-socked.

PAISLEY (n) Mental disorder, the most obvious symptom of which ii the habit of parading indoors with an open umbrella.

ORME (adj) Long-jawed, open-mouthed, vacant; hence, opposed to the televising of Parliament.

PENHALIGON (n) A quandary or dilemma occasioned by the sudden opportunity to pronounce on television about a subject on which one has no views of any kind.

PYM (n) The gift-wrapped halfpenny piece which MPs traditionally present to the Chief Clerk of Convenience In Ordinary at the end of each Parliamentary session. (Originally a unit of currency, equal to approx 7 Weetch's, 9 Dubs, 4.7 Viggers or 3 Trippiers.)

RIFKIND (n) An expression of self-righteous or insincere outrage following a public tragedy, emanating from the Prime Minister and echoed by the Leader of the Opposition; cllql, a silent fart.

SILKIN (n) The ancient Haitian art of psychoanalysing Life Peers by studying their choice of titles.

SPROAT (v) To communicate by spitting through the teeth.

SUMMERSKILL (n) The last full working day before the August Recess, traditionally a time for heavy-handed practical jokes in the Chamber, such as the placing of a whoopee cushion under the Woolsack (Sproat, 1976), the unwilling circumcision of Norman St John Stevas (Skinner, 1979) or the new system for calculating the number of unemployed (Tebbit, 1982).

VARLEY (n) A Member who is constantly mistaken for someone else, even at home (cf BEITH).

WELLBELOVED (adj) Friendless, alone, unable to attract a barman's attention even by violent means.

WINNICK (n) A collective noun covering the various ways in which people in public life conceal the fact that they need to blow their nose but haven't got a handkerchief or tissue: viz the act of burying one's head in one's hands as if in thought, or offering to take over the tea-cloth for a moment, or running the thumb and forefinger down the outside of the nose as if 'twere an udder before placing the hand face-down on the upholstery.

Contd. from page 67

DAY 16 Patient starts course of Russian for beginners. Uses door frame to make splints for crippled Ostrich.

DAY 17 First major setback—crippled ducks in territorial dispute with crippled pink flamingos.

DAY 18 Cell window now a mecca for World Ornithological Society. Patient changes name by deed poll to Joe Stalin.

DAY 19 The most crucial test of the experiment—patient is shown photograph of Norman Tebbit and immediately throws up all over the crippled Swan.

DAY 20 Straight-jacket and eggshells removed. Patient confirmed cured.

DAY 21 Patient released and padded cell handed over to the National Trust.

EPILOGUE Two weeks after his release Mr X moved to live in the rock solid Labour constituency of Bedwelty where he now actively supports Neil Kinnock MP.

KINNOCKISM—IS THERE A CURE?

During the fervour of the run-up to

THINGS I STILL DON'T KNOW AT 67

Denis Healey, the Labour member for Leeds East, is a former Chancellor of the Exchequer and Minister of Defence. His hobbies include showing people his holiday photographs and wearing dinner jackets when they are not really called for.

THE RIGHT HON DENIS HEALEY

My mother was a Russian fan-dancer and my father a racing driver, but they lost everything in the Depression and went off to work down mines. Both of them died before they'd had a chance to tell me what it was they'd lost, so I suppose that's something I've been looking for all my life—a sort of emotional cuff-link if you like. What else? To be frank, I don't think there is very much I don't know: knowing everything about everything has been a sort of hobby of mine as long as I can remember and, of course, I have always had an astonishingly good memory for a man of my size. Let me think. For some reason I have never known how to cope with wet swimming trunks. My generation was brought up in an age of bathing machines, and nowadays I find it impossible to get out of my costume on a public beach without exposing at least one of my testicles. If anything, I am worse at it the older I get. In a crisis, Edna has to lend me one of her frocks until the crowds have dispersed.

So there's that. Oh yes, and I can never fold shirts properly, but that's all really. Some people tell me that I don't know how to pronounce Sowoodi Arabia, but I don't think that's very important, do you?